ABSITE™ Review, Simplified

Simplified

ARMIN KAMYAB

authorHOUSE®

AuthorHouse™
1663 Liberty Drive, Suite 200
Bloomington, IN 47403
www.authorhouse.com
Phone: 1-800-839-8640

First published by AuthorHouse 8/20/2009

ISBN: 978-1-4389-6431-7 (e)
ISBN: 978-1-4389-6430-0 (sc)

Library of Congress Control Number: 2009903422

Printed in the United States of America
Bloomington, Indiana

This book is printed on acid-free paper.

ABSITE™ is a registered trademark of the American Board of Surgery, which neither endorses nor recommends this product.

*Neither the author nor the publisher shall be held accountable for any damage incurred as a result of advice
given in this book. Any medical information contained herein is only for illustrative purposes.*

*Use of any information contained herein remains the sole responsibility of the practitioner, including but not limited to, drug
usage, drug doses, and diagnostic modalities.   This book is not a textbook, nor a manual on medical/surgical therapeutics.*

Contents

I. Basic Sciences

II. Clinical Sciences

I. Basic Sciences

Cell Biology

Fluids/Electrolytes

Hematology

Blood Products

Immunology

Inflammation & Cytokines

Nutrition

Wound Healing

Infection

Oncology

Pharmacology – *Common Medications, Antibiotics, Anesthesia*

CELL BIOLOGY

- **AB blood types** are glycolipids
- **HLA types** are glycoproteins

- In the **cell-cycle**, the G1 phase is the most variable one, and is the one that decides the cell-cycle length. Growth Factors affect this G1 phase, and cells go to the G0 phase from this G1 phase.

During the M (mitosis) phase:

- **Prophase**, centromeres attach, nucleus disappears, spindles form
- **Metaphase**, chromosomes align
- **Anaphase**, chromosomes pull apart
- **Telophase**, nuclei reform

- **Steroid hormones** bind to their receptors in the cytoplasm. After binding to steroids, it undergoes a conformational change which allows it to translocate into the nucleus.

- **Thyroid hormone** binds to its receptor in the nucleus.

- **Growth Factor** receptors are on the cell membrane (they work by activating intrinsic enzymes, which in turn causes an effect downstream in the cell).

- Guanine-Cytosine are connected by a single-bond
- Adenine=Thymine are connected by a double=bond (or Adenine=Uracil in RNA)

- Fats cannot be used for Gluconeogenesis To produce energy during starvation, they therefore undergo β-oxidation.

- cAMP activates PKA.
- DAG activates PKC.

- Myosin filaments are **thick filaments**.
- Actin filaments are **thin filaments**.
- The **Intermediate filaments** are Keratin, Desmin (muscle), and Vimentin (fibroblasts)

- Cilia and Flagella are made up of Microtubules.

- **Northern blotting** is for RNA.
- **Western blotting** is for proteins.
- **Southern blotting** is for DNA.

- The **intracellular buffering system** is the Phosphate buffer system.

- The main component of the **extracellular matrix** is collagen.

- 2/3 of the **Total Body Water** (TBW) is intracellular, and 1/3 is extracellular.
- Most of the intracellular water is in muscle, which is why men and younger patients have more TBW.

- Proteins (mainly Albumin) are responsible for the plasma-interstitial osmotic pressure gradient.
- Na^+ is responsible for the intracellular-extracellular osmotic pressure gradient.

- The **MCC** of volume overload is iatrogenic.

- 1 Liter of **0.9% NS** contains 154 mEq of both Na^+ & Cl^-.
- 1 Liter of **LR solution** contains 130 mEq of Na^+, 4 mEq of K^+, 2.7 mEq of Ca^{+2}, 109 mEq of Cl^-, and 28 mEq of Bicarb.

- 5% Dextrose in water (**D5W**) has 5g of Dextrose per 100 mL (50g / L).

- **Plasma osmolarity** = $2Na^+ + Glu/18 + Urea/2.8$

- **Free water deficit** = $0.6 \times kg \times (current\ Na^+/140 - 1)$

- Each 100 mg/dl rise in glucose causes a 3 mEq/L decrease in the measured serum Sodium.

- **Ionized (free) Calcium** increases with acidosis, since acidosis promotes Calcium dissociation from albumin.

- During an open abdominal operation, can lose up to 1 Liter of fluids per hour to evaporation, just from having exposed bowel.

- 24 hours after GI surgery, it's best to switch the IV fluids to D5W + ½ NS + 20 mEq K, because the Dextrose will stimulate insulin release, and therefore result in a.a. uptake and protein synthesis.

- Kidney fluid losses should not be replaced 1:1 because it can simply be diuresis of excess fluids.
- GI fluid losses however are isotonic, and therefore can be replaced 1:1 with isotonic fluid.

- The stomach produces 1-2 L of fluid per day.
- Bile, Pancreas, and Duodenum each produce up to 1 L of fluid per day.

- Daily potassium requirements are ~1 mEq / Kg.

- **Saliva** is the body fluid with the highest concentration of K^+.
- **Bile and Pancreatic secretions** contain a large amount of Bicarb. This amount increases if the flow of bile/pancreatic secretions increases, because it leaves less time for Carbonic Anhydrase to act on the bicarb and therefore less bicarb is reabsorbed.
- **Bile** also contains large amounts of Cl^-.
- **GI secretions**, especially from the large bowel, contain large amounts of K^+.

- Treatment of **hyperkalemia** is to first stabilize the heart with Ca^+-gluconate, then Na^+-Bicarb to alkalize (thereby causing K^+ to enter cells in exchange for H^+), and insulin with an ampule of 50% Dextrose to drive K^+ into cells.

- Treatment of **hypokalemia** is K^+ administration. Mg^+ may need to be corrected before K^+ levels will correct.

- Treatment of **hypernatremia** is slow IVF infusion to prevent cerebral edema.
- Treatment of **hyponatremia** is initially water restriction. If this fails, diuresis can be tried, but correction of the hyponatremia should occur slowly at no more than 1 mEq/hr, to prevent **central pontine myelinosis**. Hypertonic saline is only recommended for symptomatic hyponatremia.

- Breast Ca is the **MC malignant** cause of **hypercalcemia**. Avoid LR solution since it contains Ca^{+2}, and avoid Thiazides since they cause Ca^{+2} retention. Treatment is therefore 0.9% NS and Lasix. (Management of endocrine and oncological causes of hypercalcemia are discussed in their respective chapters)
- **Hypocalcemia** presents with **Chvostek's sign** and/or **Trousseau's sign**. Similar to EKG findings of hypokalemia, Mg^+ may need to be corrected before Ca^{+2} levels will correct.

- **Magnesium** imbalances have symptoms similar to Ca^{+2} imbalances: hypomagnesemia will therefore present with spasms/tingling/neuromuscular hyperactivity, and hypermagnesemia will present with lethargy.
- Even though symptoms of hypermagnesemia are similar to hypercalcemia, EKG/cardiac findings of hypermagnesemia however are similar to EKG findings of hyperkalemia. Similarly, treatment of severe hypermagnesemia should therefore begin with Ca^+-gluconate to stabilize the heart, just like with hyperkalemia.
- Hypermagnesemia is seen with renal failure and acidosis.

- Normal gap **metabolic acidosis** is due to Na^+/Bicarb losses, like with ileostomies, or small bowel fistulas.
- In metabolic acidosis, keep the pH >7.2 with bicarb.
- Rapid correction of metabolic acid-base disturbances is by the pulmonary system. Slow correction is by the renal system.

- is due to H^+ and Cl^- losses, like with chronic NG-suction.

- **Prerenal acute renal failure** results in a FeNa <1% and a urine Na^+ of <20, since most of the Na^+ will get reabsorbed in an attempt to retain water.
- The best test for azotemia is the **Fractional excretion of Sodium** ($FeNa^+$): $\mathbf{FeNa = U_{Na}/U_{Cr} \times P_{Na}/P_{Cr}}$

- **Myoglobin** is toxic to renal cells because it gets converted to **Ferrihemate** in acidic environments. Treatment is therefore alkalizing the urine, to prevent Myoglobin's conversion to Ferrihemate.

- **Tumor lysis syndrome** causes release of purines/pyrimidines and electrolytes, leading to increased serum levels of Phosphorous, Uric acid, and Potassium.
- Treatment is IVF (to dilute), allopurinol (to decrease further uric acid production), and diuretics (to decrease serum K^+ and $PO4^-$).
- Interestingly, tumor lysis syndrome results in hypocalcemia. This occurs as a result of the hyperphosphatemia, causing Calcium to precipitate in the form of Calcium-Phosphate.

- Vitamin D gets the '25-OH' in the liver (25-Hydroxylase), and the '1-OH' in the kidneys (1-Hydroxylase).

- During pancreatitis, saponification of fat can occur with free Calcium, resulting in hypocalcemia. This is one of the late **Ranson's criteria** (see *GI – Pancreas* chapter).

- Intrinsic pathway is activated by exposed collagen, pre-Kallikrein, HMW Kininogen, and clotting factor (CF) 12.
- Extrinsic pathway is activated by Tissue factor (injured cells) and CF7.

- CF7 has the shortest $t_{1/2}$.
- CF 5 & 8 activity is lost in stored blood, but is not lost in FFP.
- CF8 is the only one not made in the liver (it's made in the vascular endothelium).
- CF10 is the common point of the Intrinsic and Extrinsic pathways.
- CF13 helps in the crosslinking of fibrin.

- The activation of thrombin requires CF 5, 10, Calcium, and Platelet factor 3.
- Thrombin not only activates fibrin, but also provides a positive-feedback system by activating CF's 5 and 8.

The anti-clotting cascade players are:

- **Antithrombin 3** inactivates thrombin.
- **Protein C** degrades CF's 5 and 8, Fibrinogen, and blocks TNF production (anti-inflammatory). Protein C is Vitamin K dependent.
- **Plasmin** degrades Fibrin, and also CF's 5 and 8. Plasmin is activated by Tissue Plasminogen Activator, which is released by the endothelium.

- **Vitamin K** takes ~6 hours to work, versus FFP which is immediate but only lasts ~6 hours.

- **TxA$_2$** (thromboxane) is released from platelets and causes vasoconstriction and platelet aggregation.
- The platelet aggregation caused by TxA$_2$ is via exposure of G2b/3a receptors, Calcium release, and activation of the PIP system (thereby causing more Calcium to be released).

- **PGI2** released from the endothelium causes vasodilation and decreases platelet aggregation.

- **FFP** has all the CF's (even CF's 5 and 8, which are typically lost in stored blood), Protein C and S, and Antithrombin 3.
- **Cryoprecipitate** contains mostly von Willebrand factor (vWF) and CF8
- **DDAVP** causes vWF and CF8 to be released from the endothelium.

- PT/INR is the best marker for liver synthesis function, because all the CF's (except CF8) are made in the liver.

- Routine anticoagulation requires an ACT of 150-200.

- Incomplete hemostasis is the **MCC** of surgical bleeding.

Bleeding disorders:

- **Von-Willebrand disease** is the **MC congenital** bleeding disorder.
- vWF is made by endothelial cells, and links the Gp1b receptor on platelets to Collagen. In von Willebrand disease, vWF is either decreased or non-functional.
- Von Willebrand disease types 1 and 2 are autosomal dominant (A-D). Type 3 (the most severe one) is autosomal recessive (A-R).
- Von Willebrand disease types 1 and 3 are due to a decreased amount of vWF.
- Von Willebrand disease type 2 is due to dysfunctional vWF.

- Treatment is Cryoprecipitate or DDAVP.
- Because vWF plays a role in platelet aggregation, von Willebrand disease causes and elevated bleeding time, but normal PT/PTT.

- **Hemophilia A** is CF 8 deficiency, with an X-recessive inheritance.
- CF 8 crosses the placenta, so a newborn with Hemophilia might not initially show any symptoms thanks to CF 8's from the mother. So just because a newborn doesn't have any bleeding problems it doesn't rule out Hemophilia.
- With a hemophilic joint, do not aspirate, but rather treat with ice, CF 8 concentrate, or Cryoprecipitate.
- Hemophilia does not just present with hemarthroses, but can also present with hematuria, bleeding gums, and possibly even cerebral hemorrhage.
- Unlike Hemophilia A, treatment of **Hemophilia B** (CF 9 deficiency) is FFP, because Cryoprecipitate has mostly CF8 and vWF, and not CF9.

- **Disseminated intravascular coagulation** (DIC) is **MCly** due to sepsis, and is often initiated by Tissue Factor.
- DIC causes an increased bleeding time (due to platelet consumption), as well as an increased PT & PTT (due to CF consumption).
- Treatment of DIC is to treat the underlying cause.

- **Heparin-induced thrombocytopenia** (HIT) is caused by anti-platelet factor Ab's ("**anti-PF4 IgG**"), which not only destroys platelets, but can also cause platelet aggregation resulting in so-called "white clots".
- LMWH has less risk of HIT.
- Treatment is to discontinue Heparin, and instead try Argatroban (a direct thrombin inhibitor), or possibly Hirudin (an irreversible direct thrombin inhibitor).

- Congenital Platelet disorders include Glanzmann's thrombasthenia and Bernard-Soulier disease:
- **Glanzmann's thrombasthenia** is a GP2b/3a receptor deficiency, preventing platelets from binding to each other via Fibrin.
- **Bernard-Soulier disease** is a GP1b receptor deficiency, preventing platelets from binding to Collagen via vWF.

- Acquired platelet disorders can be due to HIT, Uremia, or certain medications (ex. PCN, Pentoxifylline, Ticlopidine, and Dipyridamole).
- Uremia affects platelet funcion by blocking platelet GP1b and GP2b3a receptors. Treatment is dialysis.
- The drugs that affect platelet function do so by either binding to platelets directly, by binding to their receptors (GP1b or GP2b3a receptors), or by decreasing ADP in the platelets. Treatment is to stop the medication.

- Prostate surgery can cause **Urokinase** release. Urokinase activates Plasmin, therefore resulting in thrombolysis and possibly excess surgical bleeding.
- Treatment is **Aminocaproic Acid**, which reversibly binds to Plasminogen and prevents further Plasminogen molecules from being activated to Plasmin.

- CF 11 deficiency (**Rosenthal's syndrome**) is rare, with an autosomal dominant inheritance. Symptoms are mild since hemostasis can occur with even just 10% of normal CF 11 levels. When it does cause problems, it can be treated with FFP.

- The best way to predict someone's bleeding risk is with an H&P.

Hypercoagulable states:
- **Factor V Leiden** is the **MC congenital** hypercoagulable state.

- Factor V Leiden is not a disease per se; it is the name of a specific mutation. In this mutation, the Leiden variant of CF 5 is resistant to inactivation by activated Protein C.

- **Hyperhomocysteinemia** is believed to be responsible for ~10% of DVT's.
- Treatment is Vitamin B12 and Folate to drive the Methionine Synthase reaction towards Methionine, thereby using up Homocysteine.

- **Protein C/S deficiency** results in decreased inactivation of CF 5.
- Proteins C and S are vitamin K dependant. As a result, patients with Protein C/S deficiency are susceptible to Warfarin-induced skin necrosis, because not only are they deficient in Proteins C and S, but by antagonizing the action of Vitamin K with Warfarin, it decreases the function of already-deficient Proteins C and S.

- **Prothrombin gene mutation** (gene mutation at position 20210A) causes an increased amount of thrombin to circulate in the blood, resulting in a thrombophilic state.

- **Antithrombin 3 (AT3) deficiency** has an autosomal dominant inheritance, and results in decreased inhibition of thrombin.
- Diagnosis is made by measuring the concentration of AT3, or by measuring the AT3-Heparin activity in a functional assay.
- AT3 deficiency predisposes to both arterial and venous thrombi, and treatment should begin with Heparin (there's often enough AT3 to complex with Heparin).
- Prior to surgical procedures, or with refractory bleeding, treatment consists of FFP (FFP contains AT3), followed by Heparin to activate this AT3.

- **Polycythemia Vera** can cause a thrombophilic state due to the thrombocytophilia. Treatment is ASA to decrease platelet aggregation. If possible, surgery should be avoided until platelet levels are <400, and Hb is <16.

- **Lupus Anticoagulant** is an anti-phospholipid Ab.
- Not everyone with lupus anticoagulant has SLE. So the lack of SLE in a patient does not exclude Lupus Anticoagulant.
- Despite causing a thrombophilic state, Lupus anticoagulant results in a paradoxical increase in PTT. In fact, an elevated PTT that is not corrected with FFP is indicative of Lupus anticoagulant.

- Causes of acquired hypercoagulable states include smoking, cancer, IBD, OCP's, R.A., and pregnancy.

Anticoagulation medications:
- **Coumadin** blocks the Vitamin K dependant Carboxylation of Glutamine-residues in CF's 2, 7, 9, and 10 (the so-called Vitamin K dependent CF's).

- **Plavix** blocks ADP-receptors on platelets.

- **Heparin** activates antithrombin 3. It is cleared by the Reticuloendothelial system, and has a $t_{1/2}$ of 60-90 minutes.
- Long-term Heparin use can cause osteoporosis and alopecia.
- Heparin does NOT cross the placenta, whereas Coumadin does.

- **Argatroban**, which we give in patients with HIT, is a **reversible** direct thrombin inhibitor. It is metabolized by the liver, and has a $t_{1/2}$ of 50 minutes.
- **Hirudin** is an **irreversible** direct thrombin inhibitor, and is the most potent direct thrombin inhibitor.

- **Ancrod** comes from viper venom. It functions as an anticoagulant by stimulating tPA release.

BLOOD PRODUCTS

- **HIV risk** in transfusions is 1 in 1-2 million.
- **Hep B or C** risk is 1 in 250-500,000 (almost 2-3 times more likely than HIV).
- All blood products have some risk of HIV and Hepatitis, except Albumin & serum globulins since these are heat-treated.

- CMV-negative blood is used in low-birthweight infants and transplant patients.

- **Chagas disease** can be transmitted via blood transfusions.

- The **MCC** of death in transfusions is ABO incompatibility due to clerical error.

- Stored blood has low 2,3-DPG, and therefore has a high affinity for O_2.

- **MC** bacterial contaminate in blood products is E. Coli.
- **MC** blood product type to be contaminated is Platelets.

Transfusion complications:

- **Acute hemolysis** is antibody-mediated (like with ABO mismatch), and presents with fever, tachycardia, and hemoglobinuria, and can lead to DIC and shock.
- Treatment is fluids, pressors, diuretics, and bicarb.

- **Delayed hemolysis** is also antibody-mediated, but here the antibodies are against minor antigens.
- Treatment is observation if the patient is stable.

- **Non-immune hemolysis** occurs from mechanical trauma, such as squeezing the blood product bag.

- **Anaphylaxis** due to a blood transfusion typially occurs due to recipient anti-IgA IgG's versus donor IgA's in a recipient who's IgA deficient.

- Urticaria is typically due to proteins in the donor blood. Treatment is the same as with any other allergy.

- **Febrile transfusion reaction** is the **MC** type of transfusion reaction. It is non-hemolytic and is due to recipient antibodies against leukocytes in the donor blood.
- Can prevent febrile transfusion reactions with leukocyte filters.

- **Transfusion-related acute lung injury** (TRALI) is also due to recipient antibodies against donor leukocytes, but instead of getting a febrile reaction, clots develop in pulmonary capillaries, causing respiratory distress.

- Hypocoagulability after massive blood transfusions may be due to dilutional hypocalcemia, since Calcium is required in the clotting-cascade.

- Massive platelet transfusions (10-20 platelet transfusions), can result in the development of anti-platelet antibodies.

- Th1 cells (helper 1 T-cells) release IL-2, which stimulates cytotoxic T-cells (cell-mediated response).
- Th2 cells release IL-4, which promotes B-cell maturation to Plasma cells (humoral response).

- **MHC-1** is found on all nucleated cells, and attaches to the CD8 receptor (found on cytotoxic T-cells).
- It is a single chain with 5 domains.

- **MHC-2** is only found on Ag-presenting cells (B-cells, Monocytes, Dendritic cells, and Natural Killer cells), and attaches to the CD4 receptor (found on helper T-cells).
- It is 2 chains, with 4 domains.

- **NK cells** recognize cells that lack self-MHC.
- They do not require antigen-presentation or prior exposure to an antigen, and are not restricted by MHC types. They can therefore independently attack tumor cells.

- IgG and IgM are so-called "**opsonins**", meaning that they fix complement, thereby activating the classic pathway.

- HIV relies on the **CXCR4** co-receptor to be taken up into a cell.

Hypersensitivity reactions:
- **Type 1** is immediate, IgE mediated (ex. Histamine release by Mast cells in allergies).
- **Type 2** is IgG/IgM reacting with cell-bound antigens (ex. ABO incompatibility).
- **Type 3** is immune complex mediated (ex. SLE or R.A.).
- **Type 4** is delayed-type, due to T-cells releasing cytokines (ex. TB skin test or contact dermatitis).

- The major source of Histamine in the blood is **Basophils**.
- The major source of Histamine in tissues is **Mast cells.**

- The **primary lymphoid organs** include the bone marrow and the thymus, and are involved in the formation and maturation of leukocytes.

- With a clean or dirty wound, **tetanus toxoid** is recommended if a patient has had <3 doses of the toxoid, or if the patient's immune status is unknown.
- **Tetanus immunoglobulin** is recommended for dirty wounds in patients who are not immunized (>5 years since their last booster) or if their status is unknown.

INFLAMMATION & CYTOKINES

Tissue injury inflammatory phase:

- Tissue injury causes **platelet activating factors** (PAF) and tissue factors to be released from the endothelium.
- Platelets bind and also release growth factors (including **TGF-β** and **PDGF**), leading to PMN and Macrophage recruitment.

- **TGF-β** is a key component of tissue repair. It is initially released by platelets, but eventually by Macrophages and other cell types.
- It is chemotactic and activates PMN's, Macrophages, and Fibroblasts.
- It also promotes angiogenesis and epithelialization.

- **PAF** is a little different in that it is not stored in cells, but rather cleaved off by phospholipases, and hence cleaved off the cell membrane.
- It stimulates other cell types, as well as the other activating factors.

- **Macrophages** are the predominant cell type 3-4 days following tissue injury, and have the dominant role in wound healing, by releasing important growth factors, and they are the largest producers of the cytokines IL-1 and TNF-α.

- **PMN's** last 1-2 days in tissues (7 days in blood).

- **Cell types in Type 1 hypersensitivity reactions**:
- **Eosinophils** have IgE receptors, and release major basic proteins which stimulate Basophils and Mast cells to release Histamine.

- **Basophils** have IgE receptors as well, and are the main source of Histamine in the blood. They are not found in tissues.

- **Mast cells** are the main cells in Type 1 reactions, and are the main source of Histamine in tissues.

Nitrous Oxide (NO):

- NO is produced from Arginine by the enzyme Nitrous Oxide Synthase.
- In cells, NO activates GC causing an increase in cGMP. cGMP in turn causes Calcium sequestration and smooth muscle dilation.
- In the body, NO does not need to be broken down, since it is excreted very rapidly by the lungs.
- (Endothelin causes the opposite smooth muscle constriction).

- **Cytokines**:
- The main cytokines in injury and infection are **TNF-α** and **IL-1**, both of which are released predominantly by Macrophages.

- **TNF-α** is a procoagulant, causes cachexia in cancer, activates Neutrophils/Macrophages, and promotes the symptoms of shock in Gram-negative sepsis (fever, tachycardia, hypotension).

- **IL-1** is similar to TNF-α. It promotes the acute phase response, and is also responsible for fever by promoting PGE2 release, which raises the thermal set-point in the hypothalamus.

- Fever in atelectasis is caused by alveolar Macrophages releasing IL-1.
- ('Hyperthermia' is different because it's not caused by endogenous pyrogens increasing the thermal set-point, and hence it does not respond to anti-pyretics)

- **IL-6** is the most potent stimulus for **Hepatic acute phase protein** release.
- The Hepatic acute phase proteins include Amyloid A, Haptoglobin, Ceruloplasmin, α-1 antitrypsin, C3, and C-reactive protein.
- Hepatic proteins that are decreased in the acute phase include Albumin and Transferrin.

- **Interferons** are released by Lymphocytes, usually in response to viral infections.
- They activate Macrophages, NK cells, and T-cells.

Cell adhesion molecules:

- L-Selectins located on Leukocytes bind to E-selectins on the endothelium, which initiates rolling.
- Integrins on Leukocytes bind to ICAM on the endothelium, which promotes anchoring and diapedesis.

Complement:

- The **classic pathway** is activated by antibody-antigen complexes (IgG or IgM antibodies only, which is why IgG and IgM are called opsonins).
- Factors C1, 2 and 4 are only found in the classic pathway.

- The **alternate pathway** is activated by bacterial endotoxins.
- Factors B, D, and Properdin are only found in the alternate pathway.

- C3 is the convergence point for both pathways, and results in opsonization of the pathogen (the process in which a pathogen is marked for ingestion by phagocytes).

- C3 and C5 are chemotactic, and both have anaphylatoxin activity (triggering degranulation of mast cells, and increasing vascular permeability).

- C5 initiates the membrane attack pathway, resulting in the membrane attack complex (C5-9).

- Magnesium is required for both pathways.

Prostaglandins:

- PGI2 and PGE2 are bronchodilators.
- PGD2 is a bronchoconstrictor.
- All Prostaglandins cause vasodilation, except PGF2.

- **ASA** is an irreversible COX inhibitor (other NSAID's are reversible), and therefore prevents Arachidonic acid from being converted to Prostaglandins, Prostacyclins, and TxA_2.
- Its antipyretic effects are due to decreased PGE2 synthesis (resulting in the inability to raise the thermal set-point in the hypothalamus).
- Its anticoagulation effects are due to decreased TxA_2 synthesis (resulting in decreased platelet aggregation and decreased vasoconstriction...).

- **Steroids** work higher up in the pathway by blocking the enzyme Phospholipase A_2, which normally coverts membrane phospholipids to arachidonic acid.

Leukotrienes:

- LTB is chemotactic.
- LTC, LTD, and LTE are slow-reacting substances of anaphylaxis. They therefore cause bronchoconstriction, as well as increased vessel permeability.

Platelet granules:

- "α-granules" contain Platelet factor 4 (promotes platelet aggregation), β-thrombomodulin (binds thrombin), PDGF (chemoattractant), and TGF (involved in tissue repair).
- "Dense granules" contain Adenosine, serotonin, and calcium.
- Other factors released by platelets include β-lysin (antimicrobial properties), and Prostaglandins (vasoconstriction).

Reactive Oxygen species (ROS):

- ROS are used by certain organelles like lysosomes to digest ingested pathogens. At high levels however, ROS can cause significant cell damage.

- The enzyme **NADPH Oxidase** produces **Oxygen radicals**, such as O_2^-.
- This enzyme is absent in Chronic Granulomatous disease, resulting in the inability of phagocytes to kill ingested pathogens.

- The enzyme **Superoxide Dismutase** (SOD) produces **hydrogen peroxide** (H_2O_2), using Oxygen radicals as substrate.

- The enzyme **Myeloperoxidase** produces **hypochlorous acid** (HOCl), using H_2O_2 as substrate

- H_2O_2 is reduced by **Catalase** to water and Oxygen.

WOUND HEALING

Wound healing phases:

- **Inflammation** (1-10 days). The cells in the inflammation phase include platelets, PMN, and Macrophages.
- Macrophages have the main role, releasing GF's and cytokines.

- **Proliferation** (5 days – 3 weeks). Fibroblasts are the predominant cell type during the proliferation phase.
- Collagen production begins at around day 7, produced mainly by Fibroblasts.
- Neovascularization also occurs during the proliferation phase.

- **Remodeling/Maturation** (3 weeks – 1 year).
- During the maturation phase of wound healing, type 3 collagen is replaced with Type 1 collagen, and cross-linking of collagen occurs. This cross-linking is what gives collagen its strength.
- There is no net collagen production, but rather replacement of the existing Collagen.
- The scar flattens and pales during the maturation phase.
- Certain agents (ex. Penicillamine) inhibit the cross-linking of collagen.

- Alpha-Ketoglutarate, Vitamin C, Oxygen, and Iron are all required for the hydroxylation of Proline residues in collagen. This hydroxylation of Proline is required for collagen cross-linking to take place.

- Scars contain proteoglycans, hyaluronic acid, and water.
- Before revising a scar, wait 1 year to allow the scar to mature.

- Lymphocytes are the last cell-type to arrive at a wound, arriving even later than Fibroblasts.

- "Fibronectin" is a noncollagenous glycoprotein that is part of the extracellular matrix. It is a chemoattractant for Macrophages, and facilitates attachment of incoming fibroblasts.

- During the **first 2 days**, **PMN's** are the predominant cell-type in a healing wound.
- **Days 3-4, Macrophages** are the predominant cell-type.
- **Days 5** and up, **Fibroblasts** are the predominant cell-type.

- The most important factor in wound healing via **primary intention** is the **tensile strength**. This relies on collagen deposition and cross-linking.
- **Tensile strength** is never the same as before the tissue injury. The maximum tensile strenght is 80% of the original strength, and is reached at around 8 weeks.

- The most important factor in wound healing via **secondary intention** is **epithelial integrity**, thereby allowing cells to migrate from the wound edges.
- Myofibroblasts are involved in wound contraction and healing via secondary intention.

- **Essentials for wound healing** include nutrients (Vitamin C and Iron), good Oxygen delivery (no smoking, fluids, supplemental Oxygen), avoiding edema (limb elevation, compression), and removing necrotic tissue in order to have good epithelial integrity.

Impediments to wound healing:

- Infected wounds have decreased Oxygen and nutrients because bacteria use it up.
- Foreign bodies retard granulation tissue formation

- Serum Albumin <3 is a risk factor for poor wound healing.
- Steroids prevent wound healing by impairing Macrophage and PMN function, as well as inhibiting collagen synthesis. (Vitamin A counteracts this negative effect of steroids)
- Radiation affects fibroblast function as well as collagen maturation.
- Cancers affect wound healing by causing malnutrition/cachexia and by consuming nutrients.

- Diseases associated with poor wound healing are mostly connective tissue disorders, such as Osteogenesis Imperfecta (type 1 collagen defect), Ehlers-Danlos syndrome, and Marfan's (fibrillin defect).

- **Keloid** formation is an autosomal dominant trait, causing collagen to protrude beyond the original scar.
- Treatment options include radiation, steroids, silicone, and pressure.
- **Hypertrophic scar** stays within the confines of the scar. Treatment is same as Keloids.

Miscellaneous:

- Norepinephrine and Epinephrine peak 1-2 days after tissue injury.

- Thyroid hormone plays no major role in tissue repair.

- The nervous system plays no role in tissue repair.

- Daily Caloric requirements are 25 kCal/kg.
- Daily protein requirements are 1 g/kg, 20% of which should be essential a.a.'s.
- Approximately 1/3 of calories should be from fat.

- In burn patients, daily caloric requirement increases to 30 kCal/kg for every % area of the body burnt, and daily protein requirement increases by 3 g/kg for every % area of the body burnt (due to high protein catabolism).

- **Glutamine** is the **MC** a.a. in the blood and tissues.
- Glutamine is the main source of nutrition for the small bowel, as well as cancer cells.
- (The large bowel uses Short-Chain F.A.'s as its main source of nutrition)

- Low albumin is a strong risk factor for post-op morbidity/mortality as well as poor wound healing. (Though CHF and renal failure are overall the **MC** risk factors affecting post-op morbidity/mortality)
- Albumin has a $t_{1/2}$ of 20 days. Prealbumin has a $t_{1/2}$ of 2 days.

- The **Respiratory quotient** is the CO_2 produced per O_2 consumed.
- It is <1 when not producing much CO_2 or using lots of O_2, hence fat usage (β-oxidation) or starving.
- Pure carb metabolism: RQ = 1
- Pure fat metabolism: RQ = 0.7
- Pure protein metabolism: RQ = 0.8

- Post-op days 0-3 are catabolic, hence resulting in a negative Nitrogen balance. This is mainly due to cortisol (but also catecholamines and glucagon) mobilizing proteins for gluconeogenesis, wound repair, and acute phase protein production.
- Post-op days 3-6 are anabolic, hence positive Nitrogen balance.

- The liver is responsible for a.a. breakdown via the **urea cycle**.
- Protein intake in liver failure must therefore be limited, because ammonia can build up.

Starvation/major stress:

- **Glycogen** stores are depleted 24-36 hours after starvation. This glycogen comes mainly from muscles and the liver.

- **Gluconeogenesis** can occur from all a.a.'s (except Leu & Ile), Lactate (Cori cycle), Pyruvate, and Glycerol.
- Overall, the main gluconeogenesis precursors are a.a.'s (more specifically Alanine) from skeletal muscle. This protein turnover is what causes a negative Nitrogen balance during starvation.

- Fat/ketones are the main source of energy during late starvation (~1 week), since protein utilization for gluconeogenesis slows down in late starvation to conserve proteins.
- This protein-conserving mechanism during late starvation does not apply during trauma or post-op, due to catecholamines and cortisol promoting protein-mobilization for gluconeogenesis.

- Patients can go up to 7 days without eating. Any longer and **TPN** should be started.
- TPN is glucose-based, whereas PPN is fat-based.
- TPN may also be necessary as a supplement to enteral nutrition in stress, because stress decreases enteral absorption.
- If possible, enteral is a preferred route of nutrition because it maintains the integrity of the enterocytes, and stimulates greater hormone release (like insulin), hence promoting anabolism. In fact, having no enteral intake over a prolonged period of time can increase enterocyte permeability and result in gut-bacterial translocation.

- Sudden discontinuation of TPN is the **second MCC** of hypoglycemia (excessive insulin administration is #1).

- The brain usually uses glucose for energy production, but in late starvation (~2 weeks) it switches to ketones.
- The heart and most muscles use F.A.'s.
- Nerves, the adrenal medulla, RBC's, and leukocytes are all obligate Glucose users.

- Refeeding after a prolonged period of starvation/malnutrition can causee hypokalemia, hypomagnesemia, and hypophosphatemia (**refeeding syndrome**), because nutrients/electrolytes get taken up too fast by starving cells.
- Under severe cicumstances, the electrolyte abnormalities in refeeding syndrome can cause cardiac dysfunctions and arrhythmias.

- Selenium deficiency can cause cardiomyopathy.
- Vitamin E deficiency can cause neuropathy.

Fat digestion:

- Fat digestion occurs with pancreatic lipase, cholesterol esterase, and phospholipase to form micelles and free F.A.'s.

- **Short & Medium-chain F.A.'s** enter enterocytes by simple diffusion and enter the portal venous system.
- **Micelles and long-chain F.A.'s** enter enterocytes by fusing with the membrane. Within the enterocytes, these form chylomicrons, and then enter the lymphatics. At this point, chylomicrons are mostly TG's.

- Chylomicrons in the blood are cleared up in the liver by the enzyme **Lipoprotein lipase** (LPL).
- The short and medium-chain F.A.'s are taken up directly by the liver.

- Within fat cells, the enzyme **Hormone-sensitive Lipase** breaks down its T.G.'s to F.A.'s and glycerol, for these to then be released into the blood to be used up throughout the body.

- The two essential F.A.'s are Linolenic (ω-3) and Linoleic acid (ω-6), which are required for Prostaglandin synthesis and are important for immune cell function.

Carb digestion:

- Carb digestion occurs not just with salivary amylase, but also with pancreatic amylase and disaccharidase.
- Glucose and Galactose are absorbed via secondary transport (Na^+-symport), whereas Fructose is absorbed via facilitated diffusion.

- Lactose is made of Glucose and Galactose.
- Sucrose is made of Glucose and Fructose.

Protein digestion:

- Protein digestion occurs via gastric pepsin, trypsin, chymotrypsin, and carboxypeptidase.

- **Trypsin** is activated from Trypsinogen by the enzyme enterokinase (which is released by the duodenum).
- Activated Trypsin then activates other pancreatic enzymes, as well as autoactivates other Trypsinogen molecules.
- The pre-activation of Trypsin is inhibited by "Trypsin inhibitor", secreted by the same pancreatic cells that secrete Trypsin.

- Smaller proteins/peptides are broken down to a.a.'s, dipeptides, or tripeptides by proteases. These are in turn absorbed by active transport.
- The 3 branched-chain a.a.'s are Leu, Ile, and Val.
- The 8 essential a.a.'s are the 3 branched-chain a.a.'s, as well as Phe, Thr, Trp, Met, and Lys.

INFECTION

- The **MCC** of immune deficiency is malnutrition.

- The stomach is virtually sterile.
- Small bowel has some gram-positive and gram-negative cocci.
- Large bowel has almost all anaerobes

- **Gram (-) sepsis** is **MCly** due to E. Coli. It is due to the Endotoxin **Lipid A**, which causes release of TNF-α from Macrophages. This TNF- α leads to the symptoms seen in sepsis.
- The endotoxin Lipid A is part of the **Lipopolysaccharide** (LPS) that is found on Gram (-) bacterial membranes.
- The other noteworthy portion of LPS is the **O-antigen polysaccharide side-chain**, which is the major surface antigen of Gram (-) bacteria, and therefore the major determinant of antigen-specificity.
- Hyperglycemia often starts just before a patient becomes clinically septic, and is due to impaired glucose utilization.

- **Abscesses** almost always contain anaerobes. They usually occur 7-10 days post-op.
- Treatment is antibiotics and drainage.

- Line infections are usually due to Staph.
- If a central line grows bugs or shows signs of infection, treatment is to remove the central line if it is not needed.

- Infection within hours post-op can only be β-**Strep** (Necrotizing Fasciitis) or **Clostridium Perfringens** (gas-gangrene, due to α-toxin, a hemolytic lecithinase exotoxin).
- In both Necrotizing Fasciitis and gas-gangrene, treatment is debridement and PCN.
- Signs of an underling necrotizing soft-tissue infection can be hyponatremia and pain out-of-proportion to physical findings. Systemic signs/symptoms are often mild.
- Fournier's gangrene is caused by mixed organisms

- Clostridium species produce the most potent exotoxins:
- C. Diff exotoxin causes pseudomembrane colitis.
- C. Botulinum exotoxin causes GI symptoms, diplopia, dysphagia, and paralysis.
- C. Tetani exotoxin causes muscle rigidity/spasms.

- In wound infections, S. Aureus is **overall** the MC organism.
- Gram (-) bacteria and anaerobes are the **MC** organisms after GI/biliary surgeries.
- E. Coli is the **MC Gram (-) bacteria** in surgical wound infections.
- Bacteroides is the **MC anaerobe** in surgical wound infections. (Apart from indicating a GI source for the infection, Bacteroides only grows in low redox states so finding it usually indicates necrosis)

- Risk factors for post-op wound infections include operations lasting >2 hours, excessive electrocautery use (tissue damage), hematoma/seroma, older age, chronic illnesses (cardiac, renal, liver), hypotension, hypoxia, malnutrition, and immunosuppressant use.

- **MC** non-surgical hospital infection is a UTI.
- **MC** infectious cause of death post-op is pneumonia.
- **MC** single bug in ICU pneumonia is S. Aureus.

- **MC** category of bugs in ICU pneumonia is Gram (-) bacilli (like Pseudomonas).

- If a patient on anti-bacterials does not improve, suspect a fungal infection.

- The 2 'non-true' fungi are Nocardia (treat with Sulfa) and Actinomycete (treat with PCN).

- Treatment of a Brown recluse spider bite is Dapsone. If it's large, a local resection with a skin graft may be required.

- Acute septic arthritis can be due to N. Gonorrhea or Staph/Strep.
- Treatment is drainage and broad-spectrum antibiotics until cultures show the causative organism.

- Peritoneal-dialysis catheter infection is **MCly** Staph/Strep.
- Treatment is intraperitoneal antibiotics. If there is peritonitis, need to remove the catheter as well. If culture grows a GI bug (ex. Bacteroides), need to rule out a GI perforation.

Spontaneous Bacterial Peritonitis (SBP):

- Primary SBP is usually due to decreased host defenses, rather than a transmucosal infection. (SBP due to transmucosal infection would be called a secondary bacterial peritonitis).
- Low protein content in peritoneal fluid is a risk factor for SBP (ex. ascites in patients with cirrhosis).
- **MC** bug in SBP is E. Coli, though cultures are often negative. Diagnosis is therefore not from cultures, but rather from the PMN count in the ascites (PMN count of >500 cells/mL in the ascites is diagnostic).
- Treatment is with a third-generation Cephalosporin (like Ceftriaxone).
- If it does not improve despite antibiotics or if it's polymicrobial, look for a source of the infection, such as an abscess or a GI perforation.

- **Hepatitis C** infects 1-2% of the population.
- A chronic Hep C infection occurs in 60% of Hep C cases. Cirrhosis occurs in 15% of cases, and HCC in 1-5%.
- It is rare to have fulminant hepatic failure as a result of Hep C.

HIV:

- HIV risk is 70% from receiving HIV-positive blood, 30% in an infant born to an infected mother, 1% from mucus membrane contact with the virus, and 0.3% from a needle stick with a contaminated needle.
- Seroconversion occurs 1-3 months post-exposure. AZT and Lamivudine need to be given within 1-2 hours of exposure to decrease the risk of seroconversion.

- **MCC** of laparotomy in HIV is due to opportunistic infections (such as perforation due to CMV colitis).
- Neoplasia is the second **MCC** of laparotomy in HIV patients (**MCly** stomach lymphoma, followed by rectal lymphoma).

- Upper GI bleed in HIV: suspect stomach lymphoma or Kaposi's sarcoma
- Lower GI bleed in HIV: suspect CMV colitis or rectal lymphoma

- CD4 count of <200 is where we start seeing opportunistic disease.
- PCP prophylaxis should therefore be started when CD4 <200. In the presence of oral thrush or unexplained fevers, prophylaxis should be started regardless of the CD4 count.
- PCP prophylaxis is with oral Bactrim, or aerosolized Pentamidine in patients with sulfa allergies.

ONCOLOGY

- Cancers are the 2nd **MC** cause of death in the U.S. (lung Ca being the **MCC** of cancer-related deaths)
- **MC** cancer overall in women is breast, and in men, prostate.

- **PET scans** detect fluorodeoxyglucose molecules.

- **NK cells** can independently attack tumor cells (whereas T-cells require MHC recognition).
- Tumors infiltrated with lymphocytes have a better overall prognosis than those without lymphocyte infiltration, especially in melanoma, renal cell Ca, and breast Ca.
- In fact, can even do a lymphocyte transplant ("adoptive immunotherapy") as an adjuvant therapy in the treatment of cancer.

- γ-**INF** is approved for the treatment of **hairy cell leukemia**.

- Tumor antigens are usually random, except when the tumor is virus-induced.

- **Tumor markers**:
- CEA for Colon Ca
- AFP for Liver Ca
- CA-199 for Pancreatic Ca
- NSE for small cell lung Ca and neuroblastoma
- B-hCG for testicular Ca and choriocarcinoma

- CEA and PSA have $t_{1/2}$ of 18 days, so don't expect an immediate decrease after a prostatectomy.
- AFP has a $t_{1/2}$ of 5 days, so don't expect an immediate decrease after liver Ca resection.

- **EBV** is a retrovirus, associated with Burkitt's lymphoma and Nasopharyngeal Ca.

- Immunodeficiency is associated with certain cancers, (ex. Kaposi's sarcoma and GI lymphoma associated with HIV).

- Tissue damage seen with **Radiation therapy** is via direct small DNA breaks, as well as indirect DNA damage via oxygen radicals (so get maximum damage with high oxygen levels).
- The M-phase of the cell cycle is the most vulnerable to Radiation therapy, because that's when the DNA is most vulnerable to damage.
- Larger tumors require more radiation. This is why tumor debulking prior to radiation often helps to decrease the amount of radiation required in order to be effective.
- Higher-Energy radiation does not necessarily affect the skin, since the higher energy is only reached after it reaches deeper structures.

- Radiation therapy is intermittent to allow:
- Repair of normal cells
- Oxygen build up
- Redistribution of cells through the cell cycle (i.e. allow cells to get to the M-phase)

- **Radiosensitive** tumors include: Seminomas and Lymphomas
- Radiosensitive organs include: lungs, liver, lymphocytes, and kidneys

- **Radioresistant** tumors include: Epithelial and Sarcomas
- Large tumors are not very responsive to Radiation because they have a low O_2 content

- Cell-cycle specific chemotherapy medications exhibit a plateau in their killing abilities, because only a given number of cells at any given time are in the cell-cycle.
- Cell-cycle nonspecific chemotherapy medications on the other hand have a linear killing response.

- **Acrolein** is the active metabolite of **Cyclophosphamide**.
- Side-effects of Cyclophosphamide include hemorrhagic cystitis, SIADH, and gonadal dysfunction.
- **MESNA** can help with the hemorrhagic cystitis by inactivating Acrolein.

- **Levamisole** is an anti-helminthic drug that also has immune stimulating properties. It is occasionally used as an adjunct in the treatment of certain cancers (ex. Colon Ca).

- **Methotrexate** (as well as Trimethoprim) blocks the enzyme DHFR, hence blocking THF synthesis, and in turn blocking DNA synthesis.
- We can give **Leucovorin**/Folinic Acid with Methotrexate to replenish Folate, since Folinic Acid doesn't need the enzyme DHFR to get converted to Folate.

- **5-FU** blocks the enzyme Thymidylate Synthase, hence blocking dTMP synthesis, and in turn blocking DNA synthesis.

- The cardiac effects seen with **Doxorubicin** are due to O_2 radicals

- The Chemotherapy medications that cause the least bone marrow suppression are: Bleomycin, Busulphan, Vincristine, and Cisplatin.
- For those that do cause bone marrow suppression, G-CSF can be given to help stimulate the bone marrow. One of the side-effects of G-CSF includes "**Sweet's Syndrome**" (acute febrile neutropenic dermatitis).

- In a few cases, we resect normal organs to prevent cancers: colon with FAP gene, breast with BRCA gene and family history, and thyroid with RET oncogene and a family history of MEN/thyroid Ca.
- (RET gene + family history = 90% chance of medullary Ca of thyroid)

Tumor suppressor genes:

- **p53**, Chr 17, normally causes cell-cycle arrest and apoptosis
- **Rb**, Chr 13, involved in cell cycle
- **Bcl**, involved in apoptosis
- **APC**, Chr 5, involved in cell adhesion & cytoskeleton function (mutation associated with FAP)
- **DCC**, Chr 18, also involved in cell adhesion
- **BRCA**, involved in cell cycle and DNA repair
- **MSH-2**, involved in DNA mismatch repair (mutation associated with HNPPC)

Proto-oncogenes:

- **myc**, affects TF's
- **ras**, causes G-protein defects
- **sis**, causes defects in platelet-derived GF's
- **erb**, causes defects in epidermal GF's
- **srs**, causes defects in Tyr Kinase receptors
- **ret,** codes for a Tyr Kinase receptor (gain of function mutation is associated with Medullary Ca of the thyroid)

- **"Li-Fraumeni Syndrome"** is a rare autosomal dominant disorder due a p53 gene mutation.
- Patients with Li-Fraumeni syndrome are predisposed to childhood sarcomas, breast Ca, brain tumors, leukemias, Colon Ca, and adrenal Ca.

Environmental carcinogens:

- **Coal tar** exposure is associated with larynx, skin, and bronchial Ca
- **Naphthalene** is associated with bladder/urinary Ca
- **Benzene** is associated with Leukemia
- **Plastics/Vinyl Chloride** is associated with liver angiosarcoma, lung Ca and brain Ca

- **Supraclavicular nodes** can be involved in gastric, pancreatic, neck, breast, and lung cancers.

- **MCC** of axillary lymphadenopathy is lymphoma. Other common causes include breast and skin Ca.

- Periumbilical node lymphadenopathy (**"Sister Mary Joseph's node"**) is indicative of pancreatic Ca.

- Lymph nodes do not act as barriers. Having positive lymph nodes is therefore a sign of probable metastases.

- **MC** cancer to metastasize to bone is prostate Ca
- **MCC** of hypercalcemia due to bone metastases is breast Ca

- **MC** cancer to metastasize to the small bowel is melanoma

In clinical trials:

- Phase 1 is whether a drug is safe and calculating the dosage
- Phase 2 is if the drug is effective
- Phase 3 is whether or not it's better than what is already available
- Phase 4 is the entire period after the drug is approved and released

- **Induction therapy** is when a therapy is used as a sole treatment.
- **Primary therapy** is when 2 or more therapies are given; the first one is considered the primary therapy.
- **Adjuvant therapy** is when 2 or more therapies are given; the adjuvant therapy is given after the primary treatment to increase the chance of a cure. It can include chemotherapy, radiation, or hormones.
- **Salvage therapy** is a final treatment used in tumors that do not respond to initial chemo, in hopes of cure or at least improving the quality of life.

- **Colon Ca** metastasized to the liver has a low 5-year survival rate (25%), even if the liver metastases are successfully resected.
- That being said, Colon Ca that has metastasized to the liver still has the highest survival rate amongst metastases surgery.
- Poor prognostic factors for liver metastases from Colon Ca include: >3 metastases, CEA >200, or metastases >5cm.
- Genes associated with Colon Ca include: p53, APC, DCC, ras, and MSH-2.
- Colon Ca does not usually metastasize to bone.

- **Ovarian Ca** is one of the few tumors where surgical debulking improves Chemotherapy.
- **Krukenberg tumor** is a secondary Ovarian Ca originating from the GI tract. On Histology, these have characteristic mucin-secretin **signet-ring cells**.

- The only tumors completely curable with Chemotherapy are **B-cell Lymphomas**.

- **Mycosis Fungoides** is a cutenaous **T-Cell lymphoma**. Despite the name, it is not a fungal infection, but rather a type of non-Hodgkin's lymphoma.
- On Histology, these have characteristic **Sezary cells**.

- T-cell leukemias and lymphomas can be caused by the **Human T-Lymphotropic virus** (HTLV), an RNA retrovirus.

Lymphomas:

- Lymphomas are the **MCC** of chylous ascites.

- **Hodgkin's lymphoma** is characterized by the presence of **Reed-Sternberg cells**.
- **Nodular sclerosing** is the **MC** type.
- **Lymphocyte-predominant** has the best prognosis, whereas **lymphocyte-depleted** has the worst prognosis.

- **Non-Hodgkin's lymphoma** is usually systemic by the time of diagnosis.
- Most are B-cell lymphomas. Treatment is radiation and chemotherapy.

PHARMACOLOGY & COMMON MEDICATIONS

- **Sulfonamides** (Sulfa drugs) displace unconjugated bilirubin from Albumin in newborns, and can therefore cause hyperbilirubinemia and possibly neonatal bilirubin encephalopathy.

- **ED50** is the dose that produces a response in 50% of patients.
- **LD50** is the dose that kills 50% of patients.

- **Efficacy** is the ability of a drug to get to the plateau, whereas potency is how fast it gets there.

- **Tachyphylaxis** is tolerance to a drug after administration of just a few doses of the drug.

- If the peak of a drug is too high, need to decrease the dose.
- If the trough of a drug is too high, need to decrease the frequency.

- **Phase I metabolism**: simple demethylation, reduction/oxidation, hydrolysis.
- **Phase II metabolism**: glucuronidation, sulfation.

- **P450 inducers**: alcohol, cigarette, Phenobarb, Dilantin, Theophylline, Warfarin.
- **P450 blockers**: Cimetidine, Allopurinol, Calcium-channel blockers (Verapamil, Amiodarone), MAOIs, Disulfiram and antibiotics (Erythromycin, Isoniazid, Ketoconazole, Ciprofloxacin, Metronidazole).

- The P450 system can transform safe aromatic hydrocarbons into harmful carcinogens.

- **Cholestyramine** sequesters bile acids and inhibits fat absorption, and therefore results in a decreased absorption of fat-soluble vitamins.

- **ASA** poisoning initially causes tinnitus and headaches, followed by respiratory alkalosis, and eventually metabolic acidosis.

Antiemetic medications:

- **Promethazine** (Phenergan) works by blocking Dopamine receptors (just like Haloperidol), and hence can cause Tardive Dyskinesia after prolonged use. This effect can be counteracted with Diphenhydramine.

- **Metoclopramide** (Reglan) also works by blocking Dopamine receptors. It is mainly used to increase gastric motility in patients with gastroperesis, but also has some anti-nausea effects like Phenergan.

- **Ondansetron** (Zofran) works by blocking Serotonin receptors.

Cardiovascular drugs:

- **Digoxin** blocks Na^+/K^+ ATPase and eventually results in an increase in calcium in myocardial cells, thereby increasing myocardial contractions. It also has some AV-node blocking properties.
- It decreases blood flow to the bowel, and therefore has the potential to cause mesenteric ischemia.
- Hypokalemia potentiates the effects of Digoxin, causing either AV-block or arrhythmias.
- Digoxin is not cleared with dialysis; in cases of toxicity, treatment is therefore Digibind and Potassium.

- **Procainamide** is a class 1a antiarrhythmic agent.

- It can cause lupus-like symptoms, pulmonary fibrosis, QT prolongation, and Torsades de Pointes.
- Treatment of Torsades de Pointes is to discontinue Procainamide and infuse Magnesium Sulfate.

- **ACE inhibitors** are the single best agents to reduce mortality in CHF. They are also good at preventing the renal effects of HTN or DM.

- **β-blockers** are good for patients with Left Ventricular failure, because they increase filling time (preload), and also decrease the risk of MI and A. Fib post-op.

- **Vasopressin** (ADH/DDAVP) acts on V1 receptors to cause vasoconstriction, thus increasing arterial blood pressure.

ANTIBIOTICS

- **Antiseptics** kill and inhibit organism growth on living objects
- **Disinfectants** kill and inhibit organisms growth on inanimate objects
- **Sterilization** kills all organisms

- Iodophors like Betadine work poorly against fungi
- Chlorhexidine (Hibiclens) work well against fungi

- **Ribosome 30s inhibitors** include Tetracyclines, Aminoglycosides, and Linezolid
- **Ribosome 50s inhibitors** include Macrolides, Clindamycin, and Chloramphenicol
- All Ribosome blockers are bacteriostatic except Aminoglycosides and Linezolid, which are bactericidal.

- **Quinolones** block DNA helicase/gyrase. They are bactericidal.
- They are effective against most bacteria (including Staph & Pseudomonas), but not very effective against anaerobes.

- **Metronidazole** is selectively taken up by anaerobes and certain protozoa.
- It causes oxygen radical formation, and therefore exerts its effects via DNA damage.

- **Sulfonamides** are para-aminobenzoic acid (PABA) analogues, and therefore block purine synthesis.
- **Trimethoprim** (as well as Methotrexate) blocks DHFR, hence blocking THF synthesis, which in turn blocks purine synthesis

- **Penicillin resistance** is via a plasmid for β-lactamase (plasmid-transfer is overall the **MC** method of antibiotic resistance).
- **MRSA/VRE resistance** is via a mutation in a cell-wall binding-protein.
- **Gentamicin** resistance is via a mutation leading to decreased active transport.

- Vancomycin levels should peak at 20-40, and trough at 5-10
- Gentamycin levels should peak at 6-10, and trough at less than 1

- Ampicillin/Amoxicillin are more or less the same as PCN, but also work against Enterococci.

- Bacteriostatic antibiotics (ex. Tetracyclines) antagonize the effects of β-lactams.

- 1st generation Cephalosporins: -azolin, -alexin (ex. Cef azolin)
- 2nd generation Cephalosporins: -oxitin, -otetan, -uroxime (ex. Cef oxitin)
- 3rd generation Cephalosporins: -triaxone, -tazidime, -epime, -otaxime (ex. Cef triaxone)

- Cefazolin is good for prophylaxis because of its long $t_{1/2}$.
- To be effective for procedural prophylaxis, it needs to be given within 2 hours of incision.

- The antibiotics effective against **Enterococcus** include: Ampicillin/Amoxicillin, Ticarcillin/Piperacillin, Vancomycin, Aminoglycosides (synergistic with Ampicillin), and Linezolid.

- The antibiotics effective against **Pseudomonas** include: Ticarcillin/Piperacillin, 3rd generation Cephalosporins, Aminoglycosides, Carbapenems (Meropenem/Imipenem), and Fluoroquinolones.

- The antibiotics effective against **Anaerobes** include: Clindamycin, Chloramphenicol, and Metronidazole.

Antibiotic side-effects:

- (+) Coombs test with 1st generation Cephalosporins
- Prolonged QT with 2nd generation Cephalosporins
- Cholestatic jaundice/gallbladder sludging with Ceftriaxone and IV Erythromycin
- Carbapenems (Meropenem/Imipenem) lower the seizure threshold
- Nephrotoxicity and Ototoxicity with Aminoglycosides and Vancomycin (hence the reason for checking Gentamycin and Vancomycin levels)
- HTN with Vancomycin
- Peripheral Neuropathy with Metronidazole, due to the oxygen radicals.

Antivirals:

- **Acyclovir** inhibits DNApol, and is used for HSV, VZV, and EBV.

- **Ganciclovir** is used mainly for CMV
- Side-effects include bone marrow suppression and CNS toxicity.

Anti-tuberculosis medications:

- **Isoniazid** blocks Mycolic acid synthesis.
- Isoniazid needs to be given with Vitamin B6, because it causes neuropathies and CNS effects due to Vitamin B6 depletion.

- **Rifampin** blocks RNApol.
- Cutaneous (rash, pruritis) and abdominal (diarrhea, cramps) symptoms are common with Rifampin.

- **Pyrazinamide** blocks bacterial F.A. synthesis.

- **Ethambutol** affects the mycobacterial cell wall.

- All anti-TB medications are **hepatotoxic** except Ethambutol.

Antifungals:

- **Amphotericin** binds cell wall sterols, thus affecting membrane permeability.
- Side-effects include nephrotoxicity, fever, hypokalemia, hypotension, and anemia.

- **Fluconazole** and **Ketoconazole** inhibit the enzyme 14α-demethylase, a fungal cytochrome P450 enzyme.
- They work well against many types of fungi, including Candida (except Candida *Krusei*, *Glabrata*, and *Albicans*; these require Amphotericin).

- With a severe fungal infection, or fungal sepsis, treatment is Amphotericin.

- If a patient has been on prolonged broad-spectrum antibiotics, consider adding an antifungal.

ANESTHESIA

Inhaled agents:

- Lipid soluble drugs are more potent, and therefore require a smaller minimum anesthetic concentration (MAC).

- N_2O is the fastest acting inhaled agent, but has a low potency/high MAC.
- N_2O has minor myocardial depression effects.

- Most inhaled agents cause myocardial depression, increase cerebral blood flow, and decrease renal blood flow.

- **Halothane** is slow acting, but is the least intense and irritating, and is therefore good for kids. It has however the highest cardiac depression and arrhythmic effects.
- Side-effects are hepatitis/jaundice, fever, and eosinophilia.

- **Sevoflurane** is fast acting (unlike Halothane), and has less cardiac effects than Halothane.

- **Enflurane** lowers the seizure threshold.

Induction agents:

- **Thiopental** is fast acting, but decreases BP and cerebral blood flow.

- **Propofol** is also fast acting, and also causes decreased BP and cerebral blood flow.
- Propofol does not provide any analgesia.
- Do not use Propofol in patients with egg allergies, due to cross-reaction.
- Propofol is metabolized in the liver as well as in the plasma (by cholinesterases in the plasma).

- **Ketamine** causes dissociation from thalamic/limbic system, hence producing a cataleptic state (analgesia and amnesia).
- It does not cause cardio-respiratory depression, but rather causes tachycardia (due to catecholamine release) and hallucinations.
- Unlike the other induction agents, Ketamine increases cerebral blood flow, therefore avoid in patients with head injuries/or cerebral hemorrhage.

- **Etomidate** has the least hemodynamic effects, but continuous infusion of Etomidate can lead to adrenocortical suppression.

- **Rapid Sequence Intubation** is basically same as regular intubation, except that we do not wait to see if the induction agents have taken effect. We just give an induction agent and a neuromuscular blocker, and intubate.
- It is done in patients who have recently eatn, have GERD/delayed gastric emptying, are pregnant, or have bowel obstruction.

Paralytics:

- The diaphragm is the last muscle to be affected with paralytics, and is the first muscle to recover.
- The face and neck muscles on the other hand are the first to be affected and the last to recover.

- **Succinylcholine** is the only clinically-used depolarizing agent.

- It works by non-competitively binding to the post-synaptic myoneural ACh-receptor, stimulating the muscle, but preventing further ACh stimulation of the muscle.
- It is fast acting with a short $t_{1/2}$ (~5 minutes), but can cause fasciculations, increased ICP, and **Malignant hyperthermia.**
- First sign of Malignant hyperthermia is an increase in end-tidal CO_2, followed by fever, tachycardia, rigidity, acidosis, hyperkalemia (K^+ leak due to depolarization).
- Treatment of Malignant hyperthermia is Dantrolene (block Calcium-release), cooling, bicarb, and glucose.
- Do not use Succinylcholine in burn patients, spinal cord injury patients, brain injury (due to its increase in ICP), trauma, or in acute renal failure (due to the hyperkalemia).
- Succinylcholine can worsen glaucoma by causing striated muscle contractions in the eye (increased ocular pressures).
- Cholinesterase activity can be slow in some (mostly seen in Asians), causing prolonged paralysis.

- **Nondepolarizing agents** include the "-curiums" and the "-curoniums" (ex. Atracurium).
- These work by competing with ACh in the neuromuscular junction.
- Hypothermia and hypercapnia prolong the effects of nondepolarizing agents, because low Temperatures and low pH affect Hoffman/plasma degradation.

- **Atracurium** can be used in liver and renal failure, because it mainly undergoes Hoffman degradation (i.e. spontaneous degradation in blood)
- **Mivacurium** is degraded by plasma cholinesterases
- **Rocuronium** is broken down by the liver
- **Pancuronium** is eliminated by the kidneys.

- Mivacurium and Atracurium can cause Histamine release (flushing, hypotension, etc).

- Mivacurium and Rocuronium are fast acting with a **short $t_{1/2}$.**
- Pancuronium is slow-acting and has a **long $t_{1/2}$.**

- Nondepolarizing paralytics can be reversed with AChase inhibitors (ex. neostigmine, edrophonium), because AChase inhibitors will increase ACh in the neuromuscular synapse to compete with these agents.

Local Anesthetics:
- Local anesthetics increase the action potential threshold, thus preventing Na^+ influx and blocking the propagation of nerve/pain impulses.
- Both **Esters** and **Amides** are tertiary amines.
- Esters have more allergic reactions than Amides, because they are broken down to **PABA,** which is highly allergenic.

- With Lidocaine 1%, can use up to 0.5 mL/kg.

- Infected tissues are hard to anesthetize due to the acidosis.

- In terms of length of action, Bupivacaine has the highest, Procaine has the shortest.

- Epinephrine allows more local anesthetic to be used, because it stays local.
- Avoid Epinephrine in places with poor collateral circulation (ex. penis/ear), because it can cause ischemia.

- **Lidocaine side-effects** start with CNS symptoms, and progress to cardiac symptoms.
- They start with tongue numbness, lightheadedness, visual/hearing disturbance, muscle twitching, loss of consciousness, seizures... and eventually progress to cardio-respiratory arrest (usually due to V. Fib).

Narcotics:

- Narcotics affect the body's response to CO_2, and hence cause **respiratory depression**.
- Cardiovascular effects of narcotics can include **hypotension** (Histamine release causing peripheral vasodilation), or **bradycardia** (direct inhibition of the vagus nucleus in the medulla).
- **Pupillary constriction** seen with narcotics is due to inhibition of the Edinger-Westphal nucleus in the brain.

- Narcotics are metabolized in the liver, but are eventually excreted by the kidneys. Active metabolites can therefore build-up in patients with renal failure.

- Avoid narcotics with MAOIs due to the risk of **hyperpyrexic coma**.

- **Morphine** can cause Histamine release, whereas Demerol and Fentanyl don't.
- **Fentanyl** has less cardiovascular effects than Morphine.
- Fentanyl does not cross-react with Morphine allergy.
- Fentanyl causes more muscle rigidity than Morphine, due to is rapid uptake by muscle.

- **Demerol** can cause tremors/fasciculations and convulsions.

- Sufentanil, Alfentanil, and Remifentanil are all fast-acting narcotics with short half-lives.

- Morphine lasts 2-7 hours, with a sedation dose of 0.1 mg/kg.
- Fentanyl lasts 30mins - 1 hour, with a sedation dose of 1 mcg/kg. This is because Fentanyl is highly lipophilic.

Benzodiazepines:

- Benzodiazepines are metabolized in the liver, and all cause respiratory depression.

- **Midazolam** (Versed) is short-acting and is therefore good for sedation for short procedures.
- It crosses the placenta so avoid using it during pregnancy.

- Benzodiazepine overdose is treated with **Flumazenil**, a competitive GABA-A inhibitor.
- Flumazenil can cause seizures and arrhythmias, because it blocks an inhibitory-receptor. So avoid Flumazenil in a patient who has had status epilepticus, or has elevated ICP, because it might trigger a seizure.

Epidurals/Spinals:

- **Epidural** Morphine can cause respiratory depression, whereas epidural Lidocaine can cause cardiovascular depression.
- Can treat the acute bradycardia and hypotension in epidurals with decreasing the epidural dose, giving fluids, phenylephrine, and atropine.

- Morphine is favored in lumbar epidurals (abdominal surgery), whereas Fentanyl is favored in thoracic epidurals (chest surgery), because Fentanyl has less cardiovascular side-effects than Morphine.

- Diluting the concentration of epidurals allows sparing of motor function.

- Epidurals are contraindicated in hypertrophic cardiomyopathy and cyanotic heart disease, because epidurals can cause peripheral vasodilation, and patients with those cardiac problems cannot increase their cardiac output to overcome the hypotension caused by the peripheral vasodilation.

- This peripheral vasodilation/hypotension seen with epidurals is also what causes the headache associated with epidurals. Treatment is therefore bedrest (to increase cerebral blood flow), increased fluids (to increase ICP), and caffeine (to promote cerebral vasoconstriction, to increasing ICP).

- **Spinal** anesthesia is direct injection into the subarachnoid space.
- This is also contraindicated in hypertrophic cardiomyopathy and cyanotic heart disease for same reason as epidurals.
- The spread of Spinal anesthesia is affected by the patient's position.

- Caudal blocks (in the sacrum) are good for pediatric hernias and perianal surgery.

- Both epidurals and spinals can cause hypotension (peripheral vasodilation), urinary retention, abscess/ hematoma, headaches, and neurological impairment.
- If they are higher up in the spine, they can also cause respiratory depression.

Peri/postoperative complications:

- **CHF** and **Renal Failure** are the **MC** predisposing factors of postoperative mortality.

- **Post-op MI** can be asymptomatic and without EKG changes. It can present with just hypotension, bradycardia, and arrhythmia.

- A sudden rise in endotracheal CO_2 is most likely due to alveolar hypoventilation. Treatment is increasing the tidal volume or the respiratory rate.
- A sudden drop in endotracheal CO_2 is most likely due to disconnection from ventilator, but could also be a PE or severe hypotension causing decreased pulmonary blood flow.

- An Endotracheal tube should be 2cm above the carina.

- The best way to confirm correct placement of an endotracheal tube is with **end-tidal CO_2**.

- The **MC** PACU complication is nausea/vomiting.

II. Clinical Sciences

Critical Care – *Cardiovascular, Pulmonary, Renal*

Burns

Transplant

Trauma

Plastics

Head/Neck

Endocrine – *Pituitary, Adrenal, Thyroid, Parathyroid*

Breast

Thoracic

Cardiac

Vascular

Urology

Gynecology

Neurosurgery

Orthopedics

Pediatrics

GI – *GI hormones, Esophagus, Stomach, Liver, Biliary System, Pancreas, Spleen, Small Bowel, Colorectal, Anorectal*

Hernias and Abdomen

Statistics

- The kidneys get 25% of the cardiac output, and the brain gets 15%.
- The heart only gets 5% of the cardiac output.

- The cardiac output increases with increasing HR. But after 150bpm or so, the cardiac output starts to go down due to decreased diastolic filling time.

- Increased afterload causes an automatic increase in contractility to try to overcome the increased afterload ("**Anrep effect**").
- Tachycardia also causes an automatic increase in contractility ("**Bowditch effect**").

- Due to the size difference, radial artery systolic pressures are slightly higher than aortic.

- Normal O_2 delivery to consumption ratio is 5:1. Cardiac output is adjusted to keep this ratio constant.
- The **consumption of O_2** by the body is generally independent of Oxygen supply, unless very low levels are reached, then the body will start consuming less O_2.

- 2,3-DPG, temperature increase, and increased acidity all shift the **O_2-dissociation curve** to the right, and therefore lower Hemoglobin's affinity for O_2.
- This is why there is increased 2,3-DPG production in anemia.

- **p50** is the Oxygen tension at half (50%) saturation of blood.
- Normal p50 is ~27 mmHg.

- Normal **central venous pressure** (CVP) is ~7.
- Normal **venous SaO_2** is ~70%.
- An increase in venous oxygen content is due to decreased O_2 consumption, and hence conditions such as: sepsis, cirrhosis, cyanide toxicity, hypothermia, paralysis, and coma.

- Normal **pulmonary capillary wedge pressure** (PCWP) is ~11.
- PCWP is increased with pulmonary HTN, aortic regurge, mitral stenosis, and poor LV compliance.

- A **Swan-Ganz catheter** should be placed in zone 3 of the lungs (lower lungs).
- If get hemoptysis after a Swan-Ganz placement, pull it back a little bit, inflate the balloon and increase PEEP to tamponade the pulmonary artery bleed.
- Pulmonary vascular resistance can only be measured by using a Swan-Ganz.

- Blood coming into the left heart has slightly less pO_2 than blood in the pulmonary capillaries, because venous blood from the lungs empties into pulmonary veins.

- Coronary venous blood has the lowest O_2 saturation.

- Normal **alveolar:arterial gradient** is 10-15 mmHg.

- Neurogenic shock is due to loss of sympathetic tone. Treatment is volume resuscitation, phenylephrine (sympathetic agent), and steroids if it's due to a blunt spinal trauma.

- The first thing that is seen in hemorrhagic shock is an increase in diastolic pressure, due to the compensatory increase in Sympathetic tone.

- **Acute adrenal insufficiency** is characteristically unresponsive to fluids and pressors.
- Chronic adrenal insufficiency will present with hyperkalemia and hyperpigmentation (due to the increased ACTH, which has the same precursor as Melanocortin).
- Dexamethasone is the most potent of the steroids. Cortisone is the least potent.

- **"Beck's triad"** is hypotension, jugular venous distention, and muffled heart sounds. It is seen in Cardiac tamponade.
- The first sign seen on an Echo in Cardiac tamponade is impaired diastolic filling of the Right atrium.

- The triad seen in early Gram-negative sepsis is confusion, hyperventilation/resp. alkalosis, and hyperglycemia.

- **Drotrecogin Alfa (Xigris)** is a recombinant form of activated human Protein C.
- It is used in severe sepsis, because Protein C is anti-inflammatory (blocks TNF production), antithrombotic (inactivates thrombin), and is pro-fibrinolytic.

- Signs of **fat emboli** other than hypoxia can include petechia and confusion.
- A **"Sudan red stain"** in a patient with a fat emboli may show fat in the sputum or urine.
- This **MCly** occurs with lower extremity fractures or Orthopedic procedures.

- Normal **pulmonary artery pressure** is 20-30. Suspect a PE if it's >40.

- **Intra-aortic balloon pumps** inflate during diastole (triggered by the T-wave).
- They are useful in cardiogenic shock (ex. after an MI or CABG) or in patients with refractory angina, because it decreases the afterload (deflating during systole), and also improves coronary perfusion (inflates during diastole).
- The tip of the catheter here needs to be distal to the left subclavian.
- Aortic regurgitation is a contraindication to using an intra-aortic balloon pump, because the diastolic inflation worsens aortic regurgitation.

- **Dopamine** at 0-5 ug/kg/min only acts on dopamine receptors, and hence causes renal artery dilation.
- Dopamine at 6-10 ug/kg acts on β-1 receptors (increases HR).
- Dopamine at >10 ug/kg acts on α-1 receptors (increases BP).

- **Dobutamine** at 5-15 ug/kg/min acts on β-1 receptors.
- Dobutamine at >15 ug/kg also acts on β-2 receptors.

- **Milrinone** is a PDE inhibitor, and therefore causes an increase in cAMP, resulting in increased Calcium influx into cells and increased contractility.

- **Phenylephrine** only causes vasoconstriction, since it only acts on α-1 receptors.

- **Norepinephrine** acts on all α and β receptors except β-2.
- At low doses, it only acts on β-1 receptors. At higher doses, it acts on α receptors as well.

- **Epinephrine** acts on all α and β receptors, including β-2.
- Again at low doses, it only acts on β receptors, but at higher doses, it also acts on α receptors.
- Due to the β-2, in low doses it can actually cause hypotension.

- **Isoproterenol** only acts on β receptors. It therefore basically has the same effect as low-dose Epinephrine.

- **Vasopressin** (also known as DDAVP or ADH) acts on v1 and v2 receptors.
- V1 causes vasoconstriction of vascular smooth muscles (similar to α-1).
- V2 causes water reabsorption in the collecting ducts, and also causes release of vWF and CF8 from the endothelium.

- **Sodium Nitroprusside (Nipride)** is both an arterial and a venous dilator.
- At high doses, it can cause Cyanide toxicity.
- Treatment of Cyanide toxicity is initially **Amyl Nitrite**, followed by **Sodium Nitrite**, and lastly **Sodium Thiosulfate**.
- Nitrites commonly cause **Methemoglobinemia**, where the heme group of hemoglobin is oxidized to Fe^{+3}.
- Treatment of Methemoglobinemia is **Methylene Blue**.

- **Nitroglycerin** is mainly a venodilator. It decreases cardiac workload by decreasing the preload.

- **CO** poisoning can give a normal O_2 saturation reading on pulse oximetry. Normal SaO_2 therefore does not rule out CO poisoning.
- Treatment is 100% O_2.

CRITICAL CARE - PULMONARY SYSTEM

- Compliance is the ability to stretch (elasticity is the ability to recoil).
- **Pulmonary compliance** is decreased in ARDS, pulmonary fibrosis, and pulmonary edema

- With ventilators, increase the pressure (PEEP) to improve oxygenation (by keeping alveoli open).
- Increase the respiratory rate or tidal volume to decrease CO_2.

- Parameters required to wean a patient off a ventilator include: FiO_2 <40%, PEEP 5 (physiologic), RR <24, pO_2 >60, and pCO_2 <50. Patient also needs to be off pressors, and able to follow commands.

- Can get **barotrauma** with ventilators if the lungs are non-compliant (ex. ARDS, interstitial lung disease, etc).
- Inverse I:E ratio ventilation reduces the risk of barotrauma.
- Risk for barotrauma is high if the peak lung pressure is >50 for >12 hours, or if the plateau pressure (between inspiration and expiration) is >30. In such cases, consider putting a prophylactic chest tube.

- **Vital Capacity** (VC) is max inspiration to max expiration (inspiratory reserve volume + tidal volume + expiratory reserve volume).
- **Functional residual capacity** (FRC) = expiratory reserve volume + residual volume.

- Aging typically decreases the vital capacity, and increases the functional residual capacity.

- **Obstructive lung diseases** cause an increase in the total lung capacity (TLC) due to an increase in the residual volume. They therefore have a low FEV/FRC.
- In **Restrictive lung diseases** all lung volumes are decreaesd. They therefore have a high FEV/FRC.

- **Acute respiratory distress syndrome** (ARDS) is mediated by cellular inflammatory processes and increased proteinaceous material.
- The **MCC** of ARDS is SIRS/sepsis (it is basically a pulmonary manifestation of SIRS/sepsis).

- **Chemical pneumonitis** from aspiration of gastric secretions is called "**Mendelson's syndrome**".
- **MC** sites of aspiration are the superior right lower lobe, and the posterior right upper lobe.

- The main cause of **atelectasis** is bronchial obstruction. COPD and obesity are the strongest risk factors.
- It is the **MCC** of fever in the first 2 days post-op, and can also cause tachycardia.

- **Pneumothorax** under general anesthesia will present with progressively increasing inspiratory pressure, hypoxia, hypercarbia, neck vein distention, and tracheal deviation.

- A positive "**Apnea test**" for brain death is when ventilator disconnection causes CO_2 >60.

CRITICAL CARE - RENAL SYSTEM

- **Hypotension** is the **MCC** of post-op renal failure
- >70% of nephrons have to be damaged before renal dysfunction is seen.
- **Fractional excretion of Sodium (FeNa⁺)** is the best test for azotemia: $FeNa = U_{Na}/U_{Cr} \times P_{Na}/P_{Cr}$

- **Uremic coagulopathy** is an indication for dialysis.
- In a hypotensive patient (ex. shock) who needs dialysis, do "**continuous veno-venous hemofiltration**" (CVVH) instead of dialysis.

- **Renin** is released by the Juxtaglomerular apparatus in response to either low BP, hypernatremia (indicating likely dehydration), or by β-1 stimulation.
- It converts angiotensinogen to Angiotensin 1.
- Angiotensin 1 is then converted to Angiotensin 2 by **Angiotensin converting enzyme** (ACE) in the lungs.
- Angiotensin 2 not only stimulates Aldosterone release, but also causes vasoconstriction.

- **NSAIDS** cause renal damage via renal arterial vasoconstriction, from decreased Prostaglandin synthesis.
- Aminoglycosides, Myoglobin, and contrast dyes cause direct tubular injury.

BURNS

- **1st degree** burns only involve the epidermis
- **2nd degree** burns are deep to the dermis. If they involve the superficial/papillary dermis, they are painful, blanch, and have intact hair follicles. If they involve the deeper, reticular dermis, they have decreased sensation and loss of hair follicles.
- **3rd degree** burns are deep to the subcutaneous fat, and have a leathery feel.
- **4th degree** burns are down to the bone or adjacent muscle.

- Deep 2nd degree burns need to be admitted, if they involves >10% of the body in kids/elderly, or >20% of the body in all other patients.
- 3rd degree burns affecting >5% of the body need to be admitted.

- The **Parkland formula** is LR at **4 cc / kg / % body burnt**, for the first 24 hrs, half of which should be administered within the first 8 hrs.
- This is a gross underestimation with inhalational injuries, in alcoholics, and electrical injuries.
- It is important not to use Colloids/albumin in the first 24 hours because the vasculature is leaky, and can therefore get leakage of all that albumin into the extravascular spaces, causing pulmonary edema.

- Escharotomies are indicated in circumferential burns, if there are weak pulses, and if there is impaired neurological function.
- This needs to be done in the first few hours.

- Child abuse accounts for ~15% of burns in kids, so always keep it in mind.

- **Lung injury** in burn patients occurs due to inhalation of smoke and carbon materials, not heat.
- Signs of possible lung injury include facial burns, wheezing, and dark sputum.
- Intubation is required if there is stridor, worsening hypoxia, or if there has been massive volume resuscitation.
- **Pneumonia** is the most common infection in burn wound patients, and is also the **MCC** of death if there has been inhalation injury.

- Treatment of **acid/alkali burns** is water irrigation.
- Alkalis cause liquefaction necrosis, whereas acids cause coagulation necrosis.

- Treatment of **Hydrofluoric acid burns** is to spread Calcium on the wound.

- With **Tar burns**, wipe away first with a lipophilic solvent.

- **Electrical burns** need close cardiac monitoring. They can cause rhabdomyolysis, compartment syndrome, neurological problems, GI perforation, and liver/pancreatic necrosis.
- Due to the Myoglobinuria associated with rhabdomyolysis, more IVF is required, and possibly also bicarb and mannitol for renoprotection.
- Cardiac arrest after lightning is usually due to electrical paralysis of the brainstem.

- Glucose is the best source of nonprotein calories in burn patients, since burn wounds use almost entirely glucose.

- Daily protein requirement in burn patients increases by 3 g/kg for every % area of the body burnt (due to high protein catabolism).

- **Grafting** early (1 week) decreases infection, protein loss, pain, water loss, and heat loss.
- Delay grafting in the face, palms, soles, and genital burns for at least 1 week. Also delay grafting in infections or septic/unstable patients.
- **MCC** of graft rejection is a seroma/hematoma under the graft. Can apply pressure over the graft to prevent this.

- **Split thickness grafts** (part of dermis) are more likely to survive, because imbibition and revascularization occurs more easily.
- **Full thickness grafts** (whole dermis) are less likely to survive, but are also less likely to contract, and are therefore good for face/palms/hands.

- **Burn wound infections**:
- Apply Bacitracin, Neosporin, or Sulfadiazine on burns to prevent infection.
- Prophylactic IV antibiotics are not required.
- Pseudomonas is the **MC** organism in burn wounds, followed by Staph and E. Coli.
- The higher the % of body area burnt, the higher the risk of infection (also higher risk in kids).
- The reason for burn wound infections is because granulocyte chemotaxis and cell-mediated immunity are impaired in burn patients.

- **Sulfadiazine** (Silvadene) has limited eschar penetration, and can cause Neutropenia and Thrombocytopenia.

- **Silver nitrate** also has limited eschar penetration, and can cause electrolyte imbalances, discoloration, and methemoglobinemia.

- **Mafenide sodium** has good eschar penetration (unlike sulfadiazine and silver nitrate), but can cause metabolic acidosis due to Carbonic Anhydrase inhibition (decreased bicarb absorption).
- It is painful on application, but has better coverage against Pseudomonas than sulfadiazine or silver nitrate.

- **Sepsis** from burn wounds is **MCly** due to Pseudomonas.
- HSV is the **MC** virus in burn wounds.
- The best way to diagnose a burn wound infection is taking a biopsy, rather than swabbing the wound.

Burn complications:

- Seizures due to electrolyte imbalances
- Peripheral neuropathy due to small vessel injury and demyelination
- Curling's ulcer (gastric ulcer that occurs with burns)
- Marjolin's ulcer (a **malignant** SCC in nonhealing burn wounds)
- Hypertrophic scar, occurring months after the initial burn, due to increased neovascularization. Wait a year before modifying the scar cosmetically.
- Corneal abrasions and eyelid contraction in facial burns (apply topical quinolone or gentamycin)

TRANSPLANT

- **HLA-DR** is overall the most important factor in donor-recipient matching.
- **ABO** compatibility is not required for liver transplants. In renal transplants, ABO compatibility is important, and imcompatibility will cause rejection regardless of the HLA compatibility.

- **"Crossmatching"** detects the levels of preformed Ab's by mixing recipient serum with donor HLA/lymphocytes. A positive-crossmatch would therefore cause a hyperacute rejection.
- Flow cytometry is a specific and sensitive method of doing a crossmatch.

- **Skin cancer** is the **MC** cancer following any transplant
- **Post-transplant lymphoproliferative disorder** (PTLD) is the 2nd **MC** cancer following a transplant. It is related to the EBV.
- Treatment for PTLD is stopping the immunosuppression, and possibly chemo/radiation.

Types of rejection:

- **Hyperacute** is caused by preformed antibodies. They activate the complement cascade and cause vessel thrombosis. There is no treatment for this.

- **Acute** rejection is caused by T-Cells (Type 4, or delayed-type hypersensitivity), occurring 5 days to 5 weeks post-transplant.
- The T-cells release cytokines, thereby attracting Macrophages and more T-cells. In a biopsy, we therefore have Macrophage and T-cell predominance.
- Treatment is steroids and immunosuppressants.

- **Chronic** rejection is also a type IV hypersensitivity reaction, but here we also get activation of the humoral system, and eventually end up with graft fibrosis and vascular damage.

Medications:

- **Azathioprine** inhibits purine synthesis, hence inhibiting the proliferation of T-cells. **6-Mercaptopurine** is the active metabolite of Azathioprine, formed in the liver.
- **Mycophenolate** (CellCept) also inhibits purine synthesis.

- **Cyclosporin** inhibits genes for cytokine (IL-2) synthesis in Th1-cells by binding to the **cyclophilin protein**.
- This decrease in IL-2 prevents activation of resting T-cells (but has no effect on already-activated T-cells).
- Side-effects include Nephrotoxicity, HTN, tremors/neurotoxicity, hirsutism, and hyperkalemia.
- Cyclosporin undergoes hepatic metabolism and biliary excretion. Use should therefore be closely monitored in liver transplant patients.

- **Tacrolimus** (Prograf) binds to the **FK binding protein**. It then acts similar to Cyclosporin but is more potent.
- It is nephrotoxic; serum levels therefore need to be closely monitored.

- **Thymoglobulin** is an anti-T-cell antibody (made from Rabbit polyclonal antibodies). It relies on the complement system to work, because it kills T-cells via the complement pathway.

- **OKT3** (Muromonab) is a monoclonal antibody that blocks the antigen-recognition function of T-cells (by blocking the T-cell receptor complex).
- It also relies on the complement pathway and therefore requires a functional complement system.
- The effects of Muromonab can be monitored by following peripheral CD3 cell counts.

- **Zenapax** is a human monoclonal antibody against IL-2 receptors.

Kidney transplantation:

- Kidneys can be stored for up to 2 days.
- Kidney transplantation requires crossmatch and ABO compatibility.

- A UTI is not a reason not to use a donor kidney, because it can be treated.
- Even with an acute increase in creatinine (1-3) in a donor, we can still use a donor kidney.

- Donor transplantation is contraindicated if the donor has DM, HTN, or renal cancer.

Renal transplant complications:

- **Urine leaks**: treat by draining and stenting
- **Renal artery stenosis**: diagnose with U/S and treat by stenting.
- **Lymphoceles**: treat with percutaneous drainage. If recurs, consider intraperitoneal marsupialization.

- Post-operative oliguria is usually due to ATN
- Post-operative diuresis is usually due to urea and glucose
- Post-operative DM is usually due to side-effect of Cyclosporine, Prograf, or Steroids
- New proteinuria might suggest renal vein thrombosis

- In working-up kidney rejection, decrease immunosuppressants since they are nephrotoxic, and do an U/S.

- **MCC** of death in a donor is PE.
- **MC** complication in a donor is wound infection.
- Mortality post-renal transplant is usually from stroke or MI.
- The donor's remaining kidney hypertrophies due to the increased blood flow.

Liver transplantation:

- Livers can be stored for 1 day, and only need crossmatch (ABO compatibility not required).

- **Chronic Hepatitis** is the **MCC** of liver transplant in adults in the U.S.

- In some circumstances, an emergency liver transplant may be warranted, such as stupor or coma.

- Can also consider liver transplant with Hepatocellular Ca, if it is a single tumor <5cm, or up to 3 tumors, each <3cm.

- Alcohol abuse is a contraindication for liver transplantation.
- Portal vein thrombosis is not a contraindication.

- Patients with **Hepatitis B** can be given HepB Ig and Lamivudine post-operatively to prevent Hepatitis in the transplanted liver.
- **Hepatitis C** on the other hand recurs in the new liver almost every time.

- The "**APACHE score**" (used in ICU) is the best predictor of 1-year survival for liver transplants.

- **Macrosteatosis** in the donor liver is the #1 predictor of primary non-function of the transplant.
- Macrosteatosis' effect is a 1:1 ratio: if 50% of donor liver is macrosteatotic, there's a 50% chance of non-function.

- The **MC** anatomical arterial anomaly of the liver is a Right hepatic coming off of the SMA.

Liver transplant complications:

- **Bile leaks** are the **MC** liver transplant complication.
- Diagnosis and treatment is with percutaneous hepatic cholangiography +/- stent.

- **Non-function** presents with Total Bilirubin >10, PT/PTT 1.5× normal, hyperkalemia, mental status change, and increased LFTs.
- It usually requires re-transplantation.

- **Hepatic artery thrombosis**, diagnosis and treatment is with angiography +/- stent.
- Abscesses **MCly** occur as a result of hepatic artery thrombosis.

- **Acute liver transplant rejection** on Pathology shows vessel lymphocytosis, endotheliitis, and bile duct injury.

- **Chronic liver transplant rejection** presents with disappearing bile ducts. The gradually obstructing bile ducts increase the ALP.
- Acute rejection is the **MC** predictor of Chronic rejection.

Pancreas transplantation:

- The donor pancreas needs to have the Celiac artery and SMA with it, as well as a portal vein for venous drainage.

- **Thrombosis** is the **MC** complication of pancreas transplants.

- **Pancreas transplant rejection** is hard to diagnose, but may present with hyperglycemia (decreased insulin), leukocytosis, and elevated amylase.

Heart transplantation:

- A donor heart can be stored for up to 6 hours.

- Patients with heart transplants may get persistent **pulmonary hypertension** post-operatively. Treatment is with PGI2 to vasodilate the pulmonary vessels, or ECMO if it's severe.

- **Acute rejection** will present with vascular lymphocytosis, myocyte inflammation, and necrosis.
- **Chronic rejection** will present with vascular atherosclerosis.

Lung transplantation:

- Lungs, like the heart, can be stored up to 6 hours.

- The **MCC** of early mortality after a lung transplant is **reperfusion injury**.
- In reperfusion injury, the sudden rush of Oxygen into the lungs after a transplant is driven towards Superoxide production, by the Hypoxanthine that had built-up during pre-transplant ischemia.

- The only indication for a double-lung transplant is cystic fibrosis.

- In **acute rejection** we see vascular lymphocytosis.
- In **chronic rejection** we see "**bronchiolitis obliterans**", an irreversible obstructive lung disease where the bronchioles get plugged with granulation tissue.

TRAUMA

- Trauma deaths occur in peaks. The 1st peak is within 30 minutes of entering the ED, for which nothing can be done.
- The 2nd peak is 30 minutes to 4 hours, due to head injury.
- Head injury is the **MCC** of death after reaching the ED alive.
- Hemorrhage is the **MCC** of death within the first hour.
- The 3rd peak occurs days to weeks later, and is due to multisystem failure and sepsis.

- With fall injuries, the height at which half of patients die (LD$_{50}$) is 4 stories.

- With hemorrhage, BP is ok until 30% of the blood volume is lost.

- The **MCC** of airway obstruction in trauma is the tongue.

- Blunt injury is the **MC** type of trauma.
- The liver (not spleen) is the **MCly** injured organ in blunt abdominal trauma.

- A stable patient with blunt abdominal trauma should get a CT.
- A stable, but hypotensive, patient with blunt abdominal trauma, should get a DPL or a FAST, to see if a Laparotomy is required. A problem with DPL/FAST is that they do not show retroperitoneal bleeds.
- An unstable patient with blunt abdominal trauma should be resuscitated, and brought to the OR if unresponsive to resuscitation.

- With penetrating abdominal trauma, the small bowel is the **MCly** injured organ.
- In these cases, first explore the wound locally or with a laparoscope to see if the fascia is intact.

- If there is peritonitis, uncontrollable hemorrhage, diaphragm injury, peritoneal bladder injury, or renal/pancreas/biliary injuries, need to do a laparotomy.

- **Abdominal compartment syndrome** is due to massive fluid resuscitation, trauma, or abdominal surgery.
- Can get low cardiac output (due to IVC compression), GI malperfusion (from the low CO), low urine output (due to renal vein compression), and respiratory distress (upward displacement of diaphragm).
- Treatment is a laparotomy to decompress.

- If there has been any sort of trauma where pressure/pulse is lost in the ED, do a thoracotomy and clamp the aorta.

- Type O blood is available immediately.
- Type-specific blood that is neither screened nor crossmatched is available fairly quickly as well, and is relatively safe, but can cause reactions due to antibodies to minor antigens.
- Avoid Rh+ blood in girls.

Head trauma:

- **Glasgow coma scale**:
- Motor total score = 6 (6 normal, 5 localizes pain, 4 withdraws from pain, 3 flexion, 2 extension, 1 no reaction)
- Verbal total score = 5 (5 normal, 4 confused, 3 inappropriate, 2 incomprehensible sounds, no sound)
- Eye total score = 4 (4 normal, 3 opens to command, 2 opens to pain, 1 does not open eyes)

- Anything less than 14 requires a Head CT. Less than 10 requires intubation.
- **Epidural hematomas** are caused by bleeding from the middle meningeal artery. These patients usually have a lucid interval before deteriorating again.

- **Subdural hematomas** are more common, and are due to bridging vein tears.
- This can be a chronic bleed due to slow venous bleeding, especially in elderly after a minor fall.

- **Intracerebral hematomas** are usually frontal or temporal, and cause significant mass effect requiring an operation.

- Diffuse axonal injury shows up better on an MRI. It has a poor prognosis, and treatment is supportive.

- If GSC is below 8, consider putting an **intracranial pressure** (ICP) monitor. Normal ICP is ~10.
- Signs of elevated ICP include decreased ventricular size, loss of sulci, nausea/vomiting, headache, neck stiffness, seizures, and **Cushing's triad** (HTN, bradycardia, and slow RR).
- An elevated ICP can also cause dilated pupils due to uncal herniation, causing ipsilateral CN3 compression.
- Peak ICP occurs 2-3 days after trauma, because that is when we get maximum brain swelling.
- Subtracting the ICP from the mean arterial pressure (MAP) gives the **Cerebral Perfusion Pressure** (CPP). The CPP needs to be above 60.
- Treatment of an elevated ICP is therefore required if >20, because otherwise it might decrease the CPP below 60.
- Decreasing the ICP can be achieved via head elevation and diuretics (decrease fluids from the brain), relative hyperventilation (vasoconstrict cerebral vessels), sedation-induced coma, or ventriculostomy with CSF drainage.
- Phenytoin can be given prophylactically to prevent ICP-induced seizures.

- **Basal skull fractures** at the anterior fossa will give raccoon eyes.
- Basal skull fracture at the middle fossa can injure CN7. If it occurs acutely, it requires an exploration. If occurs some time after a trauma, it's likely due to edema, and exploration is therefore not needed.

- **Temporal skull fractures** can injure CN's 7 and 8.
- The **MC** site for injury to CN7 is the geniculate ganglion, located in the facial canal, between the internal acoustic meatus and the stylomastoid foramen.

- Most skull fractures do not need surgery. Surgery in skull fractures is only indicated if the skull is depressed >8mm, contaminated, or if there is persistent CSF leak that is refractory to medical therapy.

Spine trauma:
- **C-1 burst fractures** are due to straight downwards force on the spine. Treatment is with a rigid collar.

- **C-2 hangman's fracture** is typically caused by hyperextension of the neck. Treatment is with traction and a halo.

- **C-2 odontoid fracture** is due to flexion, since the odontoid process is on the anterior portion of C2.
- Treatment for type 2 and 3 odontoid fractures is fusion and a halo, because type 2 and 3 odontoid fractures involve the base of the odontoid body.

- A type 1 odontoid fracture is a fracture of the odontoid body above its base, and therefore does not require treatment.

- The thoracolumbar spine is divided into 3 "columns", and if more than one of these columns is disrupted, the spine is considered unstable.
- The anterior column has the anterior longitudinal ligament and the anterior half of the vertebral body.
- The middle column has the posterior half of the vertebral body as well as the posterior longitudinal ligament.
- The posterior column has the rest: spinous processes, lamina, etc.

- With an upright fall, there is a risk of fracture to the calcaneus, lumbar spine, and wrist/forearm.

- If there are neurological symptoms but no signs of bone injury, do an MRI because it can be ligamentous injury.

- Indications for emergency spine surgery include a spinal fracture/dislocation that's not reducible, acute anterior spinal syndrome, open fracture, compression of the cord, or progressively worsening neurological symptoms.

Maxillofacial trauma:

- **Le Fort 1** is a straight maxillary fracture. Treat with reduction and intramaxillary fixation.
- **Le Fort 2** is lateral to the nose, under the eyes, and diagonal towards the maxilla. Treatment is same as with Le Fort 1.
- **Le Fort 3** is the lateral orbital walls. Treat with suspension wiring to stabilize the frontal bone.

- **Ethmoidal-orbital fractures** will commonly present with CSF leak. Treatment is conservative initially, as most will heal.
- If there is continued CSF leak, can try an epidural catheter to decrease the CSF pressure, but ultimately these patients might need surgical closure of the dura.

- With **orbital blowout fractures**, if there is impaired upward gaze or diplopia, surgical repair with restoration of the orbital floor is required (possibly using a bone graft).

- For refractory posterior **nosebleeds**, try balloon tamponading first. If this fails, may need to embolize the internal maxillary artery or ethmoidal artery.
- Most nosebleeds originate anteriorly in the nasal cavity.

- A "**tripod fracture**" is a fracture of the zygomatic bone. Treatment is an ORIF, mainly for cosmesis.

- **Mandibular fractures** can be treated with an ORIF or metal arch bars between the top and bottom teeth.

Neck trauma:

- Asymptomatic blunt trauma to the neck requires a CT scan.
- Symptomatic blunt trauma to the neck (shock, hematoma, lost airway, subcutaneous air, stridor, hemoptysis) requires surgical exploration.

- Management of penetrating trauma to the neck depends on the zone:
- **Zone 1 (clavicle to cricoid)** requires angiography, bronchoscopy, esophagoscopy, and barium swallow.
- **Zone 2 (cricoid to angle of mandible)** requires surgical exploration.
- **Zone 3 (angle of mandible to base of skull)** requires angiography and laryngoscopy.

- **Esophageal injury** requires an esophagoscopy and esophagogram (radiograph). Most esophageal injuries are found with these two tests.
- The **MC** site of an esophageal perforation resulting from an EGD is at the Cricopharyngeus muscle (the weakest portion of the esophagus).
- If the leak is contained, and there are no systemic effects, then treatment is observation.
- If the leak is not contained (open perforation), it has been <24 hours since the perforation has occurred, there is minimal contamination, and the patient is stable, can do a primary repair with drains +/- intercostal muscle flap around the perforation.
- Otherwise if >24 hours since the perforation, if there is contamination, or if the patient is unstable, a cervical esophagostomy is required to divert the food/spit, and a chest tube is required since these patients have a high leak rate.

- **Larynx/trachea injuries** are airway emergencies, so the first step in management is therefore to secure an airway.
- A primary repair can be attempted, but most will still need a tracheostomy to allow the edema to subside.

- For Thyroid gland injuries, the first step in management is to control the bleeding.

- With **Recurrent laryngeal nerve injury**, can try to repair or reimplant it. The patient will likely still have hoarseness though.

- Vertebral artery bleeding can be controlled with ligation or embolization without any major consequences.

Chest trauma:

- After inserting a **chest tube**, if there is >1500cc of fluid upon insertion, or there is active bleeding and the patient is unstable, a thoracotomy is required.
- If a hemothorax is not drained, it can cause a fibrothorax, or an infected hemothorax.

- If a patient's oxygenation gets worst after chest tube placement, it might possibly be due to tracheal or bronchial injury.
- Diagnosis is with a bronchoscopy. If there is an injury to the trachea or bronchi, need to do a thoracotomy.
- Right bronchial injuries are more common.

- **Diaphragm injuries** are more common on the left side, and can occur from blunt trauma.
- If it has been <1 week since the injury, can repair the diaphragmatic injury through an abdominal approach. Otherwise a thoracic approach is warranted.

- A traumatic tear of the thoracic aorta usually occurs at the ligamentum arteriosum.
- Initial treatment is to control the blood pressure.
- Aortic transections are commonly associated with 1st and 2nd rib fractures.

- In **cardiac contusions**, SVT is the **MC** type of arrhythmia, but V-tach/V-fib is the **MCC** of death.
- Cardiac contusions are associated with sternal fractures.

- A flail chest usually requires at least 2 broken ribs.

- With penetrating injuries in the window between the clavicles, the xiphoid, and the nipples, need to do a pericardial window, bronchoscopy, esophagoscopy, and a barium swallow.
- If there is blood in the pericardial window, repair the heart injury and place a pericardial drain.
- With penetrating injuries outside this area, management includes possible intubation and possible chest tube, depending on the airway and pulmonary status (ex. Pneumothorax).

Pelvic trauma:

- If there is a pelvic fracture with hemodynamic instability, but negative FAST/DPL, treat by stabilizing the pelvis, and doing an angiogram.
- If FAST/DPL is positive, then need a laparotomy.

- With evidence of a pelvic hematoma, only do a laparotomy if it results from a penetrating trauma, if it's expanding, or if the patient is unstable.

- Anterior pelvic fractures are more likely to have venous bleeding, whereas posterior pelvic fractures are more likely to have arterial bleeding.

Small bowel trauma:

- The small bowel is the **MC** organ injured with penetrating injuries to the abdomen.
- Lacerations need to be repaired transversely, to avoid strictures.
- If a laceration involves more than half the circumference, need to resect that portion.

- With duodenal injuries, the 2nd portion of the duodenum is **MCly** injured.
- Most duodenal injuries can be repaired with debridement and primary closure.
- If it's an extensive injury and involves the 2nd portion, may need to do a gastrojejunostomy (pyloric exclusion).
- Death as a result of duodenal injury is **MCly** due to shock. Morbidity is **MCly** due to fistulas.

- A small bowel hematoma can present with symptoms of SBO. They have a "stacked coins" appearance on an UGI.
- Most of these hematomas can be managed conservatively.

Liver trauma:

- If less than half of the bile duct circumference is injured, can repair over a stent. Otherwise will need a choledochojejunostomy.

- **Portal vein injuries** require repair, since injury to the portal vein is associated with a high mortality rate. May need to do a pancreatectomy to get to the injured portion of portal vein.

- Surgery for liver trauma is mostly to control bleeding (ex. unstable despite resuscitation). A liver resection is rarely necessary in liver trauma.
- To control bleeding from the liver, can try perihepatic packing, which controls most bleeds up to small arterial bleeds.

- For retrohepatic IVC injuries, can do an atriocaval shunt to control the bleeding while repairing it.

Spleen trauma:

- Initial management is conservative, including strict bed rest for 5 days.

- If there is a pseudoaneurysm in the spleen, or there is active bleeding, need a splenectomy.

- Post-splenectomy sepsis is most common within 2 years after a splenectomy.

Pancreas trauma:

- Pancreatic injuries are **MCly** due to penetrating injuries (blunt trauma injuring the pancreas is less common).

- A distal pancreatic duct injury requires a distal pancreatectomy.
- A pancreatic head injury that is not surgically reparable can be treated with ERCP stenting, and drain placement.
- All pancreatic hematomas need a laparotomy.

- **"Kocher maneuver"** is dissection of the lateral peritoneal attachments of the duodenum, allowing access to the pancreas.

- With a persistently elevated amylase, consider the possibility of a missed pancreatic injury.

- Initial pancreatic injuries are not well diagnosed with a CT scan. CT scans are more sensitive for delayed signs of pancreatic injury (peripancreatic edema, necrosis...).

Colon trauma:

- The ascending and transverse colon can be repaired with primary anastomoses.
- The descending colon typically requires a colostomy.

- All paracolonic hematomas, regardless of the type of trauma, need a laparotomy.
- Colon injuries have a 10% abscess rate, and a 2% fistula rate.

Rectal trauma:

- Rectal injuries can be repaired primarily, with sacral drainage, +/- colostomy.
- Low rectal injuries can be treated transanally.

Vascular trauma:

- Major vascular injuries (pulsatile hematoma, absent pulse, ischemia, etc) need surgery. Otherwise do an angiogram first to assess the extent of the vascular injury.

- When using a saphenous vein graft to repair lower extremity arterial injuries, use a saphenous vein graft from the contralateral limb to improve outflow.

- IVC repairs can be treated with a primary repair if the injury involves <50% of the circumference.

Renal trauma:

- If need be, the left renal vein can be ligated near the IVC, since it has adrenal and gonadal collaterals.

- In the renal hilum, from anterior to posterior, we have vein then artery.

- Urine extravasation does not necessarily require an emergent surgery. Surgery is reserved for hemorrhage and instability, or major urinary tract injuries.

GU trauma (bladder, ureter, urethra):

- Extraperitoneal bladder ruptures can be treated with a Foley. Intraperitoneal bladder ruptures need surgical repair.

- With small <2cm ureteral injuries, can do a primary repair over a stent. Otherwise may need to tie off the two ends of the ureter and do a percutaneous nephrostomy, until an ileal diversion can be performed later.
- Leave drains for all ureteral injuries, to assess for urine leaks.

- Significant urethral tears require a suprapubic cystostomy, followed by repair in 2-3 months.
- "**Buck's fascia**" is the layer of deep fascia covering the penis. Penile trauma requires repair if this fascia is violated.

Pediatric trauma:

- In kids, HR, RR, and mental status are the best indicators of the hemodynamic status.
- BP is a bad predictor of hemodynamic status in the pediatric population, since it's the least sensitive to hemodynamic changes.
- Normal HR in infants is 140-180, and normal RR is 30-40.

- Because of their increased body surface area in relation to their size, kids are at a greater risk of losing heat (hypothermia).

Orthopedic trauma:

- Femur fractures can result in severe bleeding.

- Orthopedic surgical emergencies include: pelvic fractures in unstable patients, spinal injuries with neurological deficits, all open fractures, and all fractures with vascular compromise.

- All knee dislocations require an angiogram.

Trauma during pregnancy:

- Pregnant women can lose up to 1/3 of their blood volume without showing any signs.

- Try to avoid a CT scan during pregnancy, unless the condition is life-threatening and a CT scan is required.

- A Lecithin : Sphingomyelin ratio of >2:1 is a good sign of fetal lung maturity.

- The **MCC** of placental abruption in trauma is shock, followed by mechanical forces. Can test for placental abruption using the "**Kleihauer-Betke test**", which tests for fetal blood in the maternal circulation.

- Uterine rupture **MCly** occurs in the posterior fundus.
- Post-partum uterine ruptures can be treated with resuscitation alone, since the contractions of the post-partum uterus will tamponade the bleed.

PLASTICS

- All races have the same number of melanocytes, just different rates of melanin production.
- Melanin produced by melanocytes is transferred to neighboring keratinocytes via melanosomes (melanin-containing organelles) using dendritic processes.

- **Langerhans cells** are the antigen-presenting cells of the skin. They originate from the bone marrow.

- Type 1 collagen is the main type of collagen in the dermis.

- Pacinian corpuscles sense pressure.
- Meissner's corpuscles sense movement.
- Ruffini's endings sense warmth.
- Krause's end-bulbs sense cold.

- **Eccrine sweat glands** are located all over the body (highest concentration in the palms and soles).
- **Apocrine sweat glands** are located in the armpits, nipples, and groin. Hydradenitis is an infection of these apocrine sweat glands.

- **Split-thickness grafts** include all of the epidermis and part of the dermis. They are more likely to survive, since imbibition and revascularization occurs more easily with split-thickness grafts.
- **Full-thickness grafts** include all of the dermis. They have less wound contraction, and are therefore better for areas like the palm and the back of the hands.

- **Imbibition** is osmotic blood supply to the skin graft (occurs during the first 3 days).
- **Neovascularization** starts around day 3.

- The **MCC** of free-flap or pedicled-flap necrosis is venous thrombosis.

- **Transverse Rectus Abdominus Myocutaneous** (TRAM) flap viability is determined most importantly by periumbilical perforators.

- **Melanomas** are not the **MC** type of skin cancer, but are the **MCC** of skin cancer-related death.
- "**Familial BK mole syndrome**" is a familial melanoma syndrome with 100% penetrance
- In Men, melanomas are **MCly** on the back, and in women they are **MCly** on the legs.
- Melanocytes are of neural crest origin.
- Lungs are the **MC** site of melanoma metastases.
- **MC** metastasis to small bowel is melanoma.
- Superficial spreading is the **MC** type.
- Lentigo is the least aggressive type.
- Nodular is the most aggressive type.
- Always need to resect clinically positive nodes in melanoma. If nodes are negative, do a sentinel node biopsy.
- With axillary node involvement, need to do a complete axillary node dissection.
- Metastases should be resected if possible.
- In regards to the appearance of the melanoma, the presence of ulceration carries the worst prognosis.
- **Clark level** 1 is melanoma in-situ. Level 2 is through the basement membrane. Level 3 is involving the dermis. Level 4 is down to the deep/reticular dermis. Level 5 is in the subcutaneous fat.

- **Basal cell carcinoma** is the **MC** malignancy in the U.S.
- Most of these are on the head/neck.
- Pathology shows peripheral palisading of nuclei and stromal retraction.
- Morpheaform type is the most aggressive type, and produces collagenase.

- **Squamous cell carcinoma** (SCC) of the skin can develop in old burns, scars, postradiation, or chronically inflamed skin… so-called "**Marjolin's ulcer**".
- Immunosuppression is a risk factor for SCC.
- "**Bowen's disease**" is intradermal SCC (considered early-stage SCC).

- <u>Soft tissue Sarcomas</u>:
- **Malignant fibrous histiosarcoma** is overall the **MC** type of soft tissue sarcoma. **Liposarcoma** is overall the **second MC** type of soft tissue sarcoma.
- In kids, **rhabdomyosarcomas** are the **MC** type of soft tissue sarcoma. Embryonal subtype is the **MC** type; Alveolar subtype carries the worst prognosis.

- Half of all sarcomas are in kids, and half are on the extremities.
- An asymptomatic mass is the **MC** presentation.
- These spread hematogenously; node metastasis is rare.
- Lungs are the **MC** site of metastases.
- Treatment is resection of at least one fascial plane, with wide margins, and chemo / radiation for high-grade tumors.

- **Head & neck sarcomas** usually occur in kids. It's hard to get good margins due to the proximity to vital structures, therefore post-op radiation is usually required.

- **Visceral and retroperitoneal sarcomas** are usually leiomyosarcomas and liposarcomas. The most important prognostic factor is the ability to completely resect the tumor.

- **PVC** and **arsenic** exposure is associated with angiosarcomas.
- **Chronic lymphedema** is associated with lymphangiosarcoma.

- **Kaposi's sarcoma** is associated with immunocompromised states; it's the **MC** cancer in AIDS patients.
- It is **MCly** in the oropharynx.
- Treatment is chemo / radiation, or surgical resection if it involves the GI tract.

- **Bone sarcomas** are usually metastatic at the time of diagnosis.
- **Osteosarcomas** are usually in kids, common around knees, and originate from metaphyseal cells.

Genetic syndromes associated with soft tissue tumors:

- **Neurofibromatosis**: CNS tumors, peripheral sheath tumors, pheochromocytomas
- **Li-Fraumeni syndrome** (p53 mutation): childhood rhabdomyosarcomas (and many other non soft-tissue tumors)
- **Tuberous sclerosis**: angiomyolipoma
- **Gardner's syndrome**: desmoid tumors, osteomas (as well as non soft-tissue tumors, including FAP and small bowel adenocarcinoma)

- <u>Miscellaneous</u>:
- **Actinic Keratosis** is premalignant skin lesions. Seborrheic keratosis is not premalignant.

- **Merkel cell Ca** is a neuroendocrine skin cancer, hence has Neuron-Specific Enolase (NSE). It is both metastatic and aggressive.

- **Glomus cell (chemoreceptors) tumors** involve nerves and vessels, and hence are painful. These are **benign**, and are most common in the fingertips and toes.

- **Desmoid tumors** are **MCly** found on the anterior abdominal wall, but can arise in any skeletal muscle.
- They are associated with Gardner's syndrome and FAP.

Erythema Multiforme:

- **Stevens-Johnson syndrome** is a less severe form of Erythema Multiforme with less (<10%) of the body affected.
- **Toxic epidermal necrolysis** is a severe form of Erythema Multiforme with more of the body affected.
- Both cause epidermal-dermal separation, and both involve mucus membranes.
- They can be caused by drugs and viruses, and treatment is simply supportive (no steroids).

- **Anterior triangle** of the neck is bordered by the SCM muscle, the sternal notch, and the lower body of the mandible. It contains the carotid sheath, and can be further divided into 4 triangles (muscular, carotid, submandibular, and submental).
- **Posterior triangle** of the neck is ordered by the SCM, the trapezoid muscle, and the clavicle. It contains CN 11, branches of the cervical plexus, as well as the brachial plexus.

- The **Phrenic nerve** and the **subclavian vein** pass anterior to the anterior scalene.
- The **subclavian artery** passes between the anterior scalene and the middle scalene.

- **CN 10** runs between the carotids and the IJ
- **CN 5** provides sensation to the face, motor to the muscles of mastication, and taste to the anterior 2/3 of the tongue.
- **CN 12** provides motor to all the muscles of the tongue except the palatoglossus.

- **Recurrent laryngeal nerve** innervates all the laryngeal muscles except the cricothyroid muscle.
- The cricothyroid muscle is innervated by the external branch of the superior laryngeal nerve.

- "**Frey's syndrome**" is when the auriculotemporal branch of the mandibular nerve, which usually carries sympathetic nerves to sweat glands and parasympathetic nerves to the parotids, gets mixed up after facial surgery (namely parotid gland surgery), causing the parasympathetic nerves to innervate the sweat glands.
- Patients present with post-prandial redness and sweating over the cheeks.

- The **thyrocervical trunk** gives off the inferior thyroid artery, the ascending cervical artery, the transverse cervical artery, and the suprascapular artery.

- A **Radical neck dissection** removes the SCM, the IJ, CN12, the ipsilateral thyroid, the omohyoid, the submandibular glands, sensory nerves C2-5, and the cervical branch of CN7.
- A **modified radical neck dissection** spares the SCM, the IJ, and the CN12.

- Metastatic head and neck tumors **MCly** metastasize to the lungs.

- A posterior neck mass is Lymphoma until proven otherwise.

- Most **oropharyngeal cancers** are SCC, with smoking and alcohol being the strongest risk factors.
- Treatment of SCC of the lip is surgical resection with a 1cm margin. Radiation is warranted if it's stage 3 or 4, if it's recurrent, or if it has metastasized.

- The lower lip is the **MC** site for an oral cavity cancer (due to sun exposure).
- Oral cancers rarely spread to lymph nodes, except for anterior tongue tumors, which have early spread to the anterior cervical chain.
- Hard palate tumors have the worst prognosis since they are hard to resect.

- **Nasopharyngeal cancer** is associated with EBV, and can present with nosebleeds or obstruction.
- **Papillomas** are overall the **MC benign** tumor of the nasopharynx.
- In kids, **lymphomas** are the **MC** nasopharyngeal tumors.
- Nasopharyngeal (and oropharyngeal) cancers metastasize to the deep/posterior cervical nodes.
- Initial treatment for nasopharyngeal cancers is radiation or surgery.

- An extremely vascular nasopharyngeal tumor is likely a nasopharyngeal angiofibroma. Initial treatment includes angiography and embolization, followed by resection.

- **Laryngeal Ca** presents with hoarseness, dyspnea, and dysphagia.
- They can be supraglottic, glottic, or subglottic.
- Supraglottic tumors spreads to the submental/submandibular nodes, whereas glottic and subglottic tumors spread to the anterior cervical nodes.
- Treatment is radiation and surgery. If it's large, need to do a laryngectomy, with a modified radical neck dissection.

- Most **salivary gland tumors** are in the parotids, and most are **benign**.
- **Pleomorphic adenoma** is the **MC benign** tumor of the salivary glands.
- **Warthin's tumor** is the second **MC benign** salivary gland tumor.
- These often present as a painless mass.
- Treatment is a superficial parotidectomy.

- **Mucoepidermoid Ca** is the **MC malignant** tumor of the salivary glands
- **Adenoid cystic Ca** is the second **MC malignant** salivary gland tumor, but is the **MC malignant** tumor of the minor salivary glands.
- These often present as a painful mass, and/or CN 7 paralysis.
- Treatment of malignant salivary gland tumors is resection of the gland, and a prophylactic modified radical node dissection.
- During a parotidectomy, CN 7 should be sacrificed if there is tumor invasion of the nerve, or preexisting facial paralysis.

- **MCly** injured nerve during a parotidectomy is not CN7, but the **Greater auricular nerve** (from C2-3, gives sensation to skin over the parotids, mastoid, and ear), hence causing numbness over the area.

- **Hemangiomas** are the **MC** salivary gland tumors in kids.

- **Chemodectomas** are vascular tumors of the middle ear. Treatment is surgical resection.

- **Acoustic neuromas** (tinnitus, hearing loss, unsteadiness) need to be treated with a craniotomy and resection.

- CSF rhinorrhea can be confirmed with lab tests, since CSF will test positive for the "tau protein".

- Most epistaxis originates anteriorly in the nasal cavity.

- **Suppurative parotitis** occurs due to dehydration, usually in the elderly, and Staph is the **MC** organism.
- Treatment is fluids, antibiotics, and drainage.

- **Sialoadenitis** is acute inflammation of the salivary glands due to obstruction of the duct, usually by a stone.
- Treatment is to incise the duct and remove the stone.

- **Peritonsillar** and **retropharyngeal abscesses** are treated with drainage. Once they are opened, they self-drain with swallowing.

- **"Ludwig's angina"** is an infection of the floor of the mouth (usually secondary to dental infections), which can spread rapidly and cause airway obstruction.

- **Dopamine** inhibits Prolactin secretion, and to a certain extent, other pituitary hormones.
- Dopamine agonist can therefore be used for certain pituitary tumors.

- In the posterior pituitary, the supraoptic nuclei release, and the paraventricular nuclei release Oxytocin.
- The primary stimulus for ADH secretion is plasma osmolarity.

- **SIADH** is **MC** after a closed head injury, but can also be caused by a neoplasm.
- Treatment is water restriction, or hypertonic saline if Na^+ is <110, or if there is symptomatic hyponatremia.
- Na^+ should not be corrected at more than 1 mEq/L/hr, to prevent central pontine myelinosis.

- All blood supply to the anterior pituitary first passes through the posterior pituitary.

- A pituitary mass that is non-functional is usually a Macroadenoma. In such a case, resection might be warranted due to the mass-effect.

- **Prolactinoma** is the **MC** pituitary adenoma. Due to the increased Prolactin, **MC** symptoms include galactorrhea and changes in libido.
- Most do not need surgery and can be treated with a Dopamine agonist like **Bromocriptine**. If Bromocriptine doesn't work or is contraindicated (ex. pregnancy), resection is required.
- Prolactinoma is part of **MEN syndrome type 1**: Hyperparathyroidism, Pancreatic endocrine tumor (**MCly** Gastrinoma), and Pituitary tumor (**MCly** Prolactinoma).

- Mortality in **Acromegaly** is usually due to cardiac complications (valve dysfunction, cardiomyopathy…).
- Somatostatin can help by inhibiting GH release, but definitive treatment is surgical resection of the pituitary adenoma, +/- Dopamine agonists.

- **Sheehan's syndrome** is caused by pituitary ischemia due to hemorrhage/hypotension post-partum.
- The **MC** presenting symptom is difficulty lactating post-partum.

- **Craniopharyngiomas** are tumors that arise at the remnant of **Rathke's pouch**.
- They may be cystic, and are often calcified.
- Treatment is surgical. A frequent post-operative complication is DI.

- "**Nelson's syndrome**" is pituitary enlargement after bilateral adrenalectomy, due to the lack of negative Cortisol feedback on the hypothalamus, hence causing increased CRH release from the hypothalamus, and therefore pituitary enlargement.
- Can also get hyperpigmentation because MSH is made from the same peptide precursor as ACTH.
- Treatment is steroids, to produce a negative feedback on the hypothalamus.

- Superior adrenal artery is supplied by the inferior phrenic artery.
- Inferior adrenal artery is supplied by the renal artery.

- Benign adenomas are common, though adrenals are also a common site for metastases. So in anyone with a known history of Cancer and an adrenal mass, do a biopsy.
- Do surgery if the mass is heterogeneous, functioning, or if it's >4cm.

- Common metastatic cancers to the adrenals include Breast, Melanoma, Renal, and Lung cancer.

Adrenal Cortex:

- All 3 zones of the adrenal cortex have the enzymes 11- and 21-hydroxylase.

- The outermost layer (zona Glomerulosa) produces Aldosterone.
- The middle layer (zona Fasciculata) produces Cortisol.
- The innermost layer (zona Reticularis) produces androgens/estrogens.

- Adrenal lymphatics drain into the subdiaphragmatic and renal lymph nodes.

- Aldosterone secretion is most strongly stimulated by Angiotensin II, but also by hyperkalemia and ACTH.

- **Congenital Adrenal Hyperplasia is MCly** due to a 21-Hydroxylase deficiency, hence pushing the substrate Progesterone towards Androgen production instead of steroid/aldosterone production.
- Symptoms therefore include precocious puberty due to all the Androgen, and also hyperkalemia and hypotension due to the lack of Aldosterone.
- Treatment is with exogenous steroids.

- **11-OH deficiency** also results in a lack of steroid production, but here we do make Aldosterone. So not only does the substrate Progesterone get pushed towards androgens production, but also to Aldosterone production.
- Symptoms are therefore precocious puberty and hypertension.
- Treatment is exogenous steroids.

- With a **17-OH deficiency**, no androgens can be produced. It therefore presents with ambiguous genitalia in males.

- **Adrenal insufficiency/Addison's disease is MCly** caused by withdrawal of exogenous steroids.
- The **second MCC** of adrenal insufficiency is autoimmune disease.
- We usually get both a decrease in cortisol and aldosterone.
- Diagnosis is made using an **ACTH stimulation test**, measuring cortisol levels after giving ACTH.
- In acute adrenal insufficiency, apart from the hypotension and hypoglycemia, can also get fever, abdominal pain, and mental status changes.
- Treatment is steroids, and also fluids.

- **Hyperaldosteronism (Conn's syndrome)** can be either primary (low Renin as a result of the increased Aldosterone) or secondary (high Renin being the cause of the high Aldosterone).
- **Primary** hyperaldosteronism is usually due to an adenoma, or sometimes hyperplasia.
- **Secondary** hyperaldosteronism is overall more common than primary. It's seen for example in renal artery

stenosis or with a renin-secreting tumor (**Bartter's syndrome**).

- To diagnose hyperaldosteronism, check urine aldosterone levels after a **salt load**: the aldosterone level, which should go down after giving salt, will stay elevated in hyperaldosteronism.
- Then check serum Renin levels to differentiate whether it's primary or secondary hyperaldosteronism.
- Can also do a '**Captopril test**' to differentiate whether it's primary or secondary hyperaldosteronism: Captopril decreases angiotensin II, and therefore decreases stimulation of the adrenals due to secondary hyperaldosteronism.
- To localize the affected gland, do an MRI/Scintigraphy, or venous sampling.
- Adenomas are more sensitive to ACTH, whereas Hyperplasia is more sensitive to angiotensin II.
- Treatment of adenomas is adrenalectomy.
- Hyperplasia on the other hand is rarely cured, though can be managed medically with potassium and Spironolactone (which blocks Aldosterone receptors).

- **Hypercortisolism** is **MCly** iatrogenic.
- A **Pituitary adenoma**/Cushing's disease is the **MC non-iatrogenic cause** of hypercorticalism.
- An **ectopic ACTH-secreting tumor** is the **second MC non-iatrogenic cause** of hypercorticalism, usually from Small cell Ca. If the primary tumor is inoperable or not found, treatment is to remove both adrenals.
- Diagnosis is with a **24-hour urine cortisol**.
- To differentiate between primary and secondary hypercortisolism: an ACTH-secreting pituitary tumor responds to a **Dexamethasone suppression test**. A lack of response to a dexamethasone suppression test is therefore indicative of either an adrenal tumor, or an ectopic ACTH-secreting tumor.
- Can also differentiate pituitary versus ectopic ACTH release, by doing a **CRH test**, which increases ACTH release from a pituitary adenoma, but not from an ectopic source.
- Pharmacological management should be tried: **Ketoconazole**, **Aminoglutethimide**, and **Metyrapone** all inhibit steroid synthesis.
- Adrenocortical adenoma, adrenocortical carcinoma (rare), and adrenal hyperplasia are also common causes.
- **Mitotane** is an adrenolytic agent. It can be used in residual, recurrent, or metastatic adrenal disease.

Adrenal Medulla:

- In catecholamine synthesis, the rate limiting step is **Tyrosine Hydroxylase**. Metyrosine blocks this enzyme.
- PNMT, which makes Epinephrine from Norepinephrine, is only found in the adrenal medulla.

- "**Organ of Zuckerkandl**", or Paraaortic bodies, are chromaffin bodies derived from neural crest, and are usually located along the aorta around the IMA or the aortic bifurcation.
- They usually regress in the fetus, but may persist and become an accessory adrenal medulla.

- **Pheochromocytomas** are associated with MEN syndrome types 2a and 2b, Tuberous Sclerosis, Neurofibromatosis type 1 (Recklinghausen's disease), and Sturge-Weber syndrome.
- Most of these affect the right adrenal. The ones that are extra-adrenal (like in the Organ of Zuckerkandl), are more likely to be malignant.
- Diagnosis is made by **urine Metanephrine/VMA tests**. Coffee, tea, α or β blockers can all give a FP urine VMA test.
- IV contrast in Pheochromocytoma can cause a hypertensive crisis.
- Preoperatively, give an α-blocker first, then a β-blocker. β-blockade alone will cause unopposed α stimulation.
- Intraoperatively, make sure to ligate adrenal vein first to prevent spilling of catecholamines.

- The Thyroid gland comes from the 1st and 2nd pharyngeal pouches.
- The 3rd and 4th pharyngeal pouches give the Parathyroid glands and the thymus.

- Superior thyroid artery is the 1st branch off the external carotid artery.
- Inferior thyroid artery (off the thyrocervical trunk), gives superior/inferior parathyroids.
- The ima artery occurs in 1% of the population, and comes from either the aorta or an innominate artery and supplies the isthmus

- The superior and middle thyroid veins drain into the internal jugular vein.
- The inferior thyroid vein drains into innominate veins.

- **Superior laryngeal nerve** gives motor to the cricothyroid muscle. It runs lateral to the thyroid, and injury to this causes loss of projection.
- **Recurrent laryngeal nerve** gives motor to all the muscles except the cricothyroid. It runs posterior to the thyroid, and injury causes hoarseness. Bilateral injury causes airway obstruction, requiring emergency tracheostomy.

- The "**Ligament of Berry**" is a posterior medial ligament. It's located close to the recurrent laryngeal nerve so be careful when dissecting it.

- Peroxidases attach or remove tyrosine (ex. T4 to T3 conversion in the periphery).

- "**Tubercle of Zuckerkandl**" (not to be mistaken with the organ of Zuckerkandl) arises from the 4th branchial cleft, and is a lateral projection from the lateral thyroid lobe.
- It can be used as a landmark to locate the recurrent laryngeal nerve.

- Parafollicular C cells are the cells that produce Calcitonin

- Resin binds to free T3. High Resin uptake therefore either means there are high amounts of T3, or low amounts of TBG.

- Stridor post-thyroidectomy, suspect hematoma. Open the incision emergently.

- **MCC** of death in Thyroid storm is high-output cardiac failure. It often occurs post-operatively in patients with undiagnosed Grave's disease.
- Treatment is β-blockers, PTU, Lugol's solution (potassium-iodine). Emergent thyroidectomy is not indicated.

- "**Wolff-Chaikoff effect**" is what we get with high doses of Iodine, which inhibits TSH's action on the thyroid, and results in more T4 and less T3.

- A Pyramidal lobe occurs in ~10% of the population, and is due to an isthmus remnant during descent.

- There could be thyroid tissue that persists in the area of the foramen cecum at the base of the tongue.
- In many patients, this is the only thyroid tissue they have.
- Symptoms include dysphagia, dyspnea, and dysphonia.
- These have a 2% malignancy risk. Treatment is therefore radioactive iodine or resection.

- **Thyroglossal duct cysts** require resection, since they are premalignant.
- During resection, need to take the midpart of the hyoid bone.

- <u>Asymptomatic thyroid nodule</u>:
- With an asymptomatic thyroid nodule, first step is to do thyroid function tests.
- If patient is hypothyroid, then the nodule is likely hyperplasia caused by excess TSH stimulation, and usually regresses after giving Thyroxine.
- If it's a "cold" nodule, do a FNA.

- If FNA shows follicular cells, it's likely Follicular Ca.
- If FNA shows Thyroid Ca.
- If FNA shows Amyloid deposition.
- In all these cases, treatment is a thyroidectomy or a lobectomy, due to the high malignancy risk.

- If FNA shows a cyst, treatment is to drain it. If it recurs, then thyroidectomy/lobectomy.
- If FNA shows colloid tissue, there's a low risk of malignancy. Thyroidectomy/lobectomy only if enlarges.

- If FNA is indeterminate, do a thyroidectomy/lobectomy.

Causes of hyperthyroidism:

- **Grave's disease** is the **MCC** of hyperthyroidism, and is due to IgG Antibodies to TSH receptors.
- Most effective treatments include radioactive iodine and thyroidectomy.

- **Single toxic goiter** occurs in young women. Diagnosis is with a thyroid scan.
- Treatment is medical, and surgical if medical fails.

- **Toxic multinodular goiter** is the **MCC** of thyroid enlargement. It's due to hyperplasia secondary to chronic TSH stimulation.
- Treatment is medical, and surgical if medical fails.

- TSH-secreting pituitary tumors as the cause of hyperthyroidism are rare.

Treatment of hyperthyroidism:

- **PTU** and **Methimazole** block the enzyme Peroxidase. Side-effects include aplastic anemia.
- Methimazole crosses the placenta hence can cause Cretinism in the newborn. PTU does not cross the placenta.

- **Thyroidectomy** should be reserved for Grave's disease, failed medical treatment, malignant-risk, large or suspicious nodules, multinodular glands, and pregnant women who are not responsive to PTU.
- Pre-operatively, we give medications until euthyroid, then start β-blockers and Lugol's solution 1 week before the surgery.
- In pregnancy, do the thyroidectomy during the 2nd trimester; 1st trimester might result in teratogenic effects, and 3rd trimester will increase risk of premature labor.

- **Radioactive iodine** for the treatment of hyperthyroidism should be reserved for failed medical therapy, and non-surgical candidates.
- Avoid radioactive iodine in kids or during pregnancy.

Thyroiditis:

- **Hashimoto's** is the **MCC** of hypothyroidism in adults.
- It's caused by both humoral and cell-mediated autoimmune disease (Microsomal **antibodies**).
- Pathology in Hashimoto's shows lymphocytic infiltrate.
- Treatment is thyroxine, or thyroidectomy if continues to grow despite thyroxine.

- **Bacterial thyroiditis** usually spreads from a URTI.
- The thyroid is tender here.
- Treatment is antibiotics. If inflammation persists, may need a thyroidectomy.

- **De Quervain's thyroiditis** is caused by a virus.
- The thyroid is tender here.
- Treatment is with steroids and ASA. If inflammation persists, may need a thyroidectomy.

- **Riedel's fibrous struma** has fibrous components that involve adjacent strap muscles and the carotid sheath.
- It can resemble Thyroid Ca or Lymphoma on a FNA, so do a biopsy.
- Symptoms are due to hypothyroidism or compression symptoms.
- Riedel's fibrous struma is associated with other fibrotic diseases, like sclerosing cholangitis.
- Treatment is steroids to decrease the fibrosis, and thyroxine if patient is hypothyroid.

Thyroid Cancer

- Thyroid Ca is the **MC endocrine malignancy** in the U.S.
- Suspect this in any patient presenting with voice changes or dysphagia.

- In a case of sudden tumor growth, suspect hemorrhaging into the nodule/tumor.

Papillary Thyroid Carcinoma:

- Papillary thyroid carcinoma is the **MC** thyroid cancer, but is also the least aggressive and slowest growing and therefore has the best prognosis.
- Risk factors include childhood radiation exposure.

- Spread is typically via **lymphatic spread**, but prognosis is based on local invasion.
- It rarely metastasizes, but when it does, the lungs are most common site of metastases.

- On pathology we see **Psammoma bodies** and **Orphan Annie nuclei**.

- Treatment is lobectomy, unless there are bilateral lesions, positive margins, or lesion >1cm, then do a total thyroidectomy.

- With positive cervical nodes, or extrathyroidal tissue involvement, need an ipsilateral modified radical neck dissection.
- A Radical neck dissection removes the SCM, the IJ, CN12, the ipsilateral thyroid, the omohyoid, the submandibular glands, sensory nerves C2-5, and cervical branch of CN7.
- A Modified radical neck dissection spares the SCM, the IJ, and CN12.

- After surgery, if there are metastases, residual local disease, or capsular invasion, then give radioactive iodine 6 weeks after surgery.
- Radiation therapy alone without surgery is reserved for tumors that are unresectable, or in non-surgical candidates.

- An enlarged lateral neck lymph node that shows thyroid tissue is Papillary tyroid Ca with lymphatic spread until proven otherwise.

Follicular Thyroid Carcinoma:

- Hematogenous spread is the **MC** method of spread for Follicular thyroid carcinoma, and **MCly** to bone, in contrast to Papillary Ca which had lymphatic spread.
- Many of these have metastasized by the time of diagnosis.

- Treatment is lobectomy. If the pathology shows adenoma or follicular cell hyperplasia, you're clear.
- If pathology shows follicular cancer, need to do a total thyroidectomy.

- Just like with Papillary thyroid carcinoma, positive cervical nodes or extrathyroidal tissue involvement requires an ipsilateral modified radical neck dissection.

- And again, like with Papillary thyroid carcinoma, if after surgery there are metastases, residual local disease, or capsular invasion, then give radioactive iodine 6 weeks after surgery.

Medullary Thyroid Carcinoma:

- Associated with **MEN syndrome types 2a and 2b**, and is usually the first presentation of MEN 2 (ex. diarrhea) and also the **MCC** of death in MEN syndrome type 2a/2b.
- It's more aggressive than Follicular and Papillary Ca, but not as aggressive as Anaplastic Ca.
- They originate from Parafollicular C cells. C-cell hyperplasia is considered pre-malignant.
- Pathology shows **Amyloid** deposition.

- Gastrin can be used to test for Medullary thyroid Ca, because it triggers an increase in Calcitonin in Medullary thyroid Ca.
- If there is an increase in Calcitonin, symptoms will include flushing and diarrhea.

- Due to the association with type 2 MEN syndrome, these patients need to be screened for Pheochromocytoma (MEN 2a and 2b) and Hyperparathyroidism (MEN 2a).

- This has lymphatic spread (like Papillary thyroid ca), and typically has early metastases to the lungs, liver, and bone.

- Treatment is total thyroidectomy with central neck node dissection.
- If the patient has positive cervical nodes, then also need a modified radical neck dissection.

- In a patient with known type 2 MEN syndrome, do a prophylactic thyroidectomy and central node dissection at age 2, since almost all of these patients will get Medullary Thyroid Ca.

- If there is already metastasis to the liver or to bone, then a thyroidectomy will not likely be curative.

- Since these involve Calcitonin releasing cells, can monitor Calcitonin levels to assess for disease recurrence.

Hürthle Cell Carcinoma:

- Most of these are **benign** adenomas, in older patients.

- Malignant ones metastasize to the bone and lung.

- Treatment is total thyroidectomy, and modified radical neck dissection if there are positive cervical nodes.

Anaplastic Thyroid Cancer:

- These present in elderly patients with long-standing goiters, and are the most aggressive of the thyroid Cancers.

- These are almost always fatal, and are often beyond surgical management by time of diagnosis.

- Can perform palliative thyroidectomy for compression symptoms.

Miscellaneous:

- **Radioactive Iodine (I^{131})** therapy is effective for Papillary and Follicular Tyroid Ca only.
- Medullary thyroid Ca does not respond to radioactive iodine therapy, since it is a tumor of Parafollicular C-cells.
- It's done 6 weeks post-operatively, because TSH levels are highest 6 weeks post-operatively, and hence greater I^{131} take-up by the thyroid gland.
- Thyroxine is not given until after I^{131} therapy is finished, because Thyroxine will suppress TSH release.
- Indications for I^{131} include tumor recurrence, inoperable tumors, metastatic disease, capsular invasion, or local extrathyroidal disease.

- Radiation therapy is effective for all but Anaplastic thyroid Ca (the most aggressive one).

- Lymphoma and SCC are very rare causes of Thyroid Ca.

ENDOCRINE - PARATHYROID

- The **Superior Parathyroids** arise from the 4th pharyngeal pouch.
- The **Inferior Parathyroids** arise from the superior portion of the 3rd pharyngeal pouch (the inferior portion of the 3rd pouch becomes the thymus).

- The **Inferior Thyroid artery** (off the Thyrocervical trunk) supplies both the superior and inferior Parathyroids.

- **MCC** of hypoparathyroidism is a previous thyroid surgery.

Primary hyperparathyroidism:

- The "**PRAD-1**" oncogene increases the risk of a parathyroid adenoma.

- Bicarb gets excreted in the urine in exchange for calcium absorption, potentially resulting in hyperchloremic metabolic acidosis.

- "**Osteitis Fibrosa Cystica**" is bone lesions due to the calcium resorption from the elevated PTH.

- Most patients have no symptoms, but rather have elevated calcium as an incidental finding.
- Those that do have symptoms, have symptoms such as: muscle weakness, myalgia, kidney stones, pancreatitis, depression/mental status change, bone pain/fractures, constipation.

- Surgery is indicated if there is symptomatic hypercalcemia, or if serum calcium levels are >13.

- Most patients with hyperparathyroidism have a simple adenoma, or hyperplasia.
- Parathyroid cancer is rare.

- With hyperplasia, don't biopsy all the glands, because of the risk of hemorrhage and hypoparathyroidism. Instead resect 3 or all 4 of the glands.

- With hyperparathyroidism during pregnancy, do the surgery during the 2nd trimester, because the hypercalcemia increases the risk of having a stillbirth if it's not treated.

- Intraoperative frozen sections can tell us whether the tissue taken was parathyroid tissue.

- Intraoperative PTH levels can help determine if the causative gland is removed, since PTH's $t_{1/2}$ is 3-5 minutes.
- Levels should go down ~50% within 10 minutes if the affected gland is removed.

- **MC** ectopic location of a parathyroid gland is in the thymus, so check inferiorly if the gland is missing.
- If still nowhere to be found, close and do a Parathyroid scan to look for the ectopic.
- **MCC** of persistent hyperparathyroidism is a missed adenoma in the neck.

- Post-operative hypocalcemia can occur, due to the remaining parathyroids not working well (low PTH levels), and also due to bones that were previously starved for calcium now taking it all up.

- If things get better for a while, but hyperparathyroidism then recurs, it's likely due to a new adenoma formation.

- With a Thallium scan, both the Thyroid and Parathyroid glands light up.

- With a Technetium scan only the Thyroid lights up.
- So when done together, it's digitally substrated to help find the Parathyroid tissue.
- (Most places however use a Sestamibi scan…)

- The **Sestamibi-Technetium scan** has preferential uptake by overactive parathyroid glands. It's therefore good for picking up adenomas, but not so much for simple hyperplasias.
- It is also the best test for picking up ectopic parathyroid adenomas.

Secondary Hyperparathyroidism:

- This is seen in patients with renal failure. It's in response to the low Calcium. No surgery is therefore needed.

- The increase in hyperparathyroid can cause aluminum accumulation in bones over time, hence causing renal osteodystrophy.

- Treatment is to prevent the secondary hyperparathyroidism, hence give Calcium, Vitamin D, and controlling Phosphate in the diet.

Tertiary Hyperparathyroidism:

- With renal failure and secondary hyperparathyroidism, after it gets corrected (ex. kidney transplant), we still have a lagging hyperparathyroidism…this is refered to as tertiary hyperparathyroidism
- We therefore have normal/high calcium levels (no longer renal failure), and a lagging high PTH.

Familial Hypercalcemic Hypocalciuria:

- This is caused by overactive PTH receptors in the DCT of the kidney, therefore resulting in increased calcium reabsorption, with normal PTH levels.
- These usually do not require treatment.

Pseudohyperparathyroidism:

- This is the opposite of FHH, in that in pseudohyperparathyroidism, the PTH receptors don't respond to PTH. We therefore get high PTH levels, yet normal/low calcium levels.

Parathyroid Cancer:

- This is a rare cause of hyperparathyroidism/hypercalcemia, but when it is present and is causing hypercalcemia, mortality is pretty high at about 50%, due to the hypercalcemia.
- Lung is the **MC** location for metastases
- Treatment is parathyroidectomy and ipsilateral thyroidectomy.

MEN Syndrome:

- These arise from "**APUD cells**", which are a type of cell that secrete hormones.

- They have an **autosomal dominant** inheritance pattern, with 100% penetrance.

- **MEN 1** affects the Pancreas (usually Gastrinoma), Parathyroid, and Pituitary (usually Prolactinoma).
- Parathyroid is usually the first to be symptomatic (hypercalcemia, often causing kidney stones).
- Treatment is to first treat the hyperparathyroidism (resect all 4 parathyroid glands).

- **MEN 2a** is Pheochromocytoma, Medullary Ca of the thyroid, and Parathyroid.
- Thyroid is usually the first to be symptomatic (diarrhea).

- Medullary Ca of the thyroid is the **MCC** of death in MEN 2.
- Treatment is to first correct the Pheochromocytoma.

- **MEN 2b** is Pheochromocytoma, Medullary Ca of the thyroid, Neuromas, and often Marfan's syndrome.
- Thyroid is the first to show symptoms.
- Treatment is to first correct the Pheochromocytoma.

Miscellaneous:

- In terms of Cancers that cause hypercalcemia: ectopic PTH release is more common than hematologic bone-destroying cancers like MM.
- An easy way to differentiate whether a cancer is causing hypercalcemia via ectopic PTH release or via bone lysis, is to measure **urinary cAMP levels**: urine cAMP levels are elevated with ectopic PTH release, due to PTH-related peptide's effect on the kidneys.

- **Mithramycin** can be used for hypercalcemia in bone metastases, as it inhibits Osteoclasts.

- For an acute hypercalcemic crisis, treatment is fluids, furosemide, +/- dialysis.

BREAST

Anatomy:

- Breast tissue is formed from ectodermal mammary bands/milk streaks.
- Estrogen promotes duct development (a double layer of columnar cells).
- Progesterone promotes lobular development.
- Both promote glandular development (this is why after menopause we get breast atrophy).

- The thoracodorsal artery (off the subscapular artery) supplies the Latissimus muscle.
- Thoracodorsal nerve innervates the Latissimus muscle.

- The **Intercostobrachial nerve** supplies the lateral cutaneous branch of the 2nd intercostal nerve, and therefore provides sensation to the medial arm/axilla.
- It runs right below the axillary vein. It can be transected during an axillary dissection without serious consequences.

- Breast blood is supplied by a mix from the intercostal arteries, internal thoracic artery, lateral thoracic, and thoracoacromial trunk
- (The thoracoacromial trunk gives off the Pectoral, Acromial, Clavicular, and Deltoid branches)

- **"Batson's plexus"** are valveless vein plexus that allow for direct hematogenous metastasis of breast Ca to the spine.

- Most breast lymph drains to the axillary nodes. ~1-2% drains to internal mammary nodes.
- Any breast quadrant can drain into these internal mammary nodes.

Benign breast diseases:

- **"Poland's syndrome"** is hypoplasia of the chest wall, amastia, hypoplastic shoulders, and hypoplastic pectorals.

- **"Mondor's disease"** is superficial vein thrombophlebitis in the breast. It is associated with trauma and strenuous exercise. Treat with NSAIDs.

- **Painful breast** is rarely breast Ca. If cyclical (before menstruation), it's usually due to Fibrocystic disease. If it's continuously painful, it's usually an acute/subacute infection.
- Treat a painful breast by first stopping caffeine and nicotine

- **Fibrocystic disease** symptoms include breast pain, possibly nipple discharge, palpable mass(es), and lumpy breast tissue.
- Irregular menses and low bodyweight are risk factors for fibrocystic disease

- **Intraductal papilloma** is the **MCC** of bloody nipple discharge.
- They are usually small and non-palpable, because they are often close to the nipple.
- They are not pre-malignant. Treatment is therefore a simple subareolar resection.

- **Fibroadenoma** is the **MC** breast lesion in young women.
- They present as painless, slow-growing, firm, rubbery masses.
- They can change in size during menses and/or during pregnancy, but are never painful. They can reach >5cm.
- On mammography, we can have large calcifications of these Fibroadenomas, especially of the lobulated type, called "popcorn lesions".
- In patients <30 years old, treat by first confirming Fibroadenoma with mammogram and/or U/S, then FNA or core needle. Avoid excisional biopsies in young women because it can affect breast development.

- In patients >30 years old, treatment is excisional biopsy to confirm Fibroadenoma.

Nipple discharge:

- Most nipple discharge is **benign**. Still, anytime a patient has nipple discharge, get a complete H&P and get a mammogram.
- Green discharge is usually fibrocystic disease.
- Bloody discharge is **MCly** from Intraductal papillomas (and occasionally ductal Ca).
- Serous discharge is usually worrisome for Ca. By-pass FNA/core-biopsy, and just do an excisional biopsy of that ductal area.
- "Spontaneous" discharge is always worrisome for Ca regardless of the color or type of discharge.

Pre-malignant conditions:

- **Diffuse Papillomatosis** has a high risk of breast Ca.
- This is when the papillomas affect multiple ducts of both breasts: "swiss cheese" appearance on mammogram.
- Diffuse papillomatosis can present with serous nipple discharge.

- **DCIS** is malignancy of the ductal epithelium but without invasion of the basement membrane.
- ~50% of DCIS will become cancer if not resected, and 5-10% will get cancer of the contralateral breast.
- Can get **Paget's disease** in DCIS.
- DCIS is usually not-palpable, so it's often only seen as calcifications on mammography.
- Since it is premalignant, need 2-3mm margins on excision.
- Treatment is lumpectomy, +/- radiation +/- Tamoxifen.
- Need to do a simple/subcutaneous mastectomy if it's a large tumor not amenable to a lumpectomy, can't get good margins, high-grade (i.e. comedo, multicentric, multifocal), or have Paget's disease. No axillary lymph node dissection is required.
- Of the different subtypes, Comedo is the most aggressive, and has the highest risk of recurrence. Treatment of Comedo is going straight to a simple/subcut mastectomy regardless of how small/big the tumor is, due to its aggressiveness.
- Low-grade DCIS also has a high risk of recurrence if the lesion is >2.5cm.

- **LCIS** is a 'marker' of breast Ca, it's not premalignant itself.
- Almost 50% of patients with LCIS get cancer of either breast (usually Ductal Ca), and 5% already have breast cancer when LCIS is diagnosed.
- This has no calcifications and is usually not palpable.
- It does not require treatment per-se, but consider bilateral subcutaneous mastectomy for prophylaxis to prevent breast cancer from arising.
- We do not need negative margins, since LCIS itself is not premalignant. It is merely a marker for other breast cancers.

Breast Cancer:

- Low socioeconomic areas have the lowest risk of breast Ca in the U.S., and Japan has the lowest rate of breast Ca in the world.
- About 12% of women in the U.S. will get breast Ca. Screening decreases mortality by 25%. If untreated, the survival rate is 2-3 years.

- ~10% of breast Ca have a negative mammogram and a negative U/S.

Symptomatic mass work-up:

- In patients **<30 years old** with a mass, do an U/S. Mammography has no value in young girls due to the dense breast content.
- If it's a solid mass, do a FNA/core-needle biopsy. Avoid excisional biopsies in young patients because it can affect the breast development.
- If however FNA/core-needle biopsy is nondiagnostic, need to do an excisional biopsy.

- In patients **30-50 years old**, get bilateral mammograms first, then do a FNA/core-needle biopsy.

- In patients **>50 years old**, get bilateral mammograms first, then do an excisional or core-needle biopsy.

- With cysts: if the cyst fluid is bloody, if it's clear but recurs, or if it's a complex cyst, then the patient needs an excisional biopsy.

- **Mammography** has a 90% sensitivity rate for picking up cancers. This increases with age since dense parenchymal tissue is replaced with fat.
- A mass needs to be >5mm to be detected on mammography.
- Screening is every 2-3 years after the age of 40, and annually after the age of 50.
- In high-risk patients, do a mammography 10 years before the youngest age of breast cancer diagnosis in a relative... unless the patient is <30 years old, because mammography in women <30 has no diagnostic value due to the dense breast tissue.
- There are mammography classifications called **Bi-RADS**: 1 is negative. 2 is benign finding. 3 is probably benign finding. 4 is suspicious abnormality. 5 is highly suggestive of malignancy.

- **"Rotter's nodes"** are lymph nodes between the pectoralis major and minor muscles.
- Only level 1 axillary lymph nodes (lateral to pectoralis minor) need sampling.
- Nodes are the most important prognostic staging factor in breast cancer (i.e. survival is directly related to the number of positive nodes).
- A node does not have to be palpable to be positive.

- Bone is the **MC** site of metastasis. Other common locations for metastases include the lungs, liver, and the brain.

- A 1 cm breast tumor most likely started ~5 years ago from a single cell.

Staging:
- T2 is 2-5cm. T3 is >5cm. T4 is any size with direct extension to the skin or chest wall (but not pectoral muscle involvement)
- N1 is 1-3 axillary nodes. N2 is 4-9 axillary nodes. N3 is 10 or more axillary nodes or any non-axillary, local nodes (infraclavicular, internal mammary).
- Supraclavicular node, even though it's local, is considered distant metastases (M1)

- Women with the greatest risk of breast Ca are those with the **BRCA gene and family history**.
- Without the BRCA gene, the greatest risk factor is having 2 or more relatives with bilateral or premenopausal breast Ca.
- After BRCA gene and family history, those with DCIS or LCIS have the greateast risk of getting breast Ca.

- Milder risk factors include: radiation, high-fat diet, obesity, first birth after the age of 30.

- BRCA 1 is also associated with Ovarian and Endometrial Ca (consider a hysterectomy and oophorectomy).
- BRCA 2 is associated with male breast Ca.

- Prophylactic mastectomy is reserved for high-risk patients: BRCA gene and family history, or LICS.

- Receptor-positive tumors are **MC** in post-menopausal women.
- Tumors positive to both Progesterone and Estrogen receptors have the best prognosis.
- Between the two, Progesterone-receptor positive tumors have a better prognosis.
- ~10% of breast Ca have neither receptors.

- Male cancer is not only associated with BRCA 2, but also steroids, family history, and Klinefelter's syndrome.
- Treatment of male Ca is a modified radical mastectomy.

Breast Cancer types:

- **Ductal Ca** accounts for ~85% of all breast Ca.
- It can have 4 different types: medullary, tubular, mucinous, and scirrhotic.
- Medullary has smooth borders, lymphocytes, and has a favorable prognosis.
- Tubular has tubule formation and has a favorable prognosis.
- Mucinous produces mucin/colloid, and has a favorable prognosis.
- Scirrhotic has the worst prognosis.
- Can get **Paget's disease** in Ductal Ca.
- Treatment for Ductal Ca is either a mastectomy, or a lumpectomy with axillary lymph node dissection/ sentinel node biopsy, +/- radiation.
- Radiation is indicated after a mastectomy if >4 nodes, skin/chest wall involvement, positive margins, >5cm tumor, inflammatory Ca, or involvement of the internal mammary nodes (N3).

- **Lobular Ca** accounts for ~10% of all breast Ca.
- It is typically bilateral/multifocal/multicentric, infiltrates extensively, and does not calcify.
- Worst prognosis is when they have "Signet ring cells".
- Treatment is the same as with Ductal Ca: mastectomy or lumpectomy with axillary node dissection/sentinel node +/- radiation.

- **Inflammatory Ca** is very aggressive with a survival rate of ~3 years.
- It commonly affects the skin and lymphatics, hence causing peau d'orange, erythema, and warm breasts.
- Treatment is a mastectomy then radiation. If it is a large tumor, first give chemotherapy and radiation to shrink the tumor, then do a mastectomy.

- **Breast Cancer management**:
- In terms of further diagnostic studies, if a patient complains of bone pain, do an ALP and bone scan to assess for bone metastases.
- If complains of headaches, obtain a head CT to assess for bone metastases.

- There are absolute contraindications to breast-conserving therapy, such as:
- 2 or more primary tumors in different quadrants
- Repeated positive margins after numerous surgical attempts
- Recurrence in the same region

- Pregnancy is an absolute contraindication to using breast irradiation. Though in the 3rd trimester, can do breast surgery, and then irradiate after delivery.

- **Sentinel node biopsy** has fewer complications than axillary node dissections.
- It's only indicated for malignant tumors >1cm, or small tumors with low risk of axillary metastases.
- Sentinel biopsy works best when the primary is identified, because then the radiotracer finds the right lymphatic channel.
- ~95% of the time, the sentinel node is found. If however can't find radiotracer or dye, need to do a formal axillary lymph node dissection.
- Don't do a sentinel node biopsy during pregnancy (due to the radiotracer), with positive nodes (requires a full axillary dissection), or with previous axillary surgery.

- Complications of axillary lymph node dissection include axillary vein thrombosis (acute swelling), lymphatic fibrosis (slow swelling, over years).
- Leave a drain in place until output is <40 cc/day.

- A **modified radical mastectomy** removes all breast tissue (including the areola and nipple), as well as axillary nodes.
- A **radical mastectomy** also removes the overlying skin, as well as the pectoralis major and minor muscles.

It is rarely done anymore.
- The Intercostal brachiocutaneous nerve is the **MCly** damaged nerve after a mastectomy. Injury to this nerve presents with hyperesthesia of the inner arm and the lateral chest wall. There are no severe consequences.

- **Radiotherapy** usually consists of 5000 rads for a lumpectomy.
- Complications of radiation therapy include rib fractures, pneumonitis, ulceration, sarcoma, and cancer of the contralateral breast.
- Scleroderma is an absolute contraindication to radiation, because it can cause severe fibrosis and necrosis.
- SLE and R.A. are relative contraindications to irradiation.
- Radiation is good for bone metastases

- With **positive nodes**, all patients should get chemotherapy except post-menopausal women who are estrogen-receptor positive; they get Tamoxifen.
- With **negative nodes** and a tumor >1cm again all patients should get chemotherapy except older patients; they get Tamoxifen.
- With **negative nodes** and a tumor <1 cm, no chemotherapy is required..
- **Tamoxifen** has a 1% risk of causing blood clots, and a 0.1% risk of causing endometrial Ca.
- Chemotherapy in breast cancer consists of Cyclosporine / Methotrexate / 5FU, or, Cyclosporine / Adriamycin. The length of treatment with either chemotherapy regimen is 3-6 months.

- Pain, swelling, and erythema in metastatic areas is called a "**metastatic flare**".

- There are some benign breast conditions that mimic Ca:
- Radial scar (irregular spiculated mass lesion)
- Fibromatosis (locally invasive spindle cells +/- skin retraction/dimpling)
- Granular cell tumors (skin retraction/dimpling)
- Fat necrosis (status post trauma), the related fibrosis can cause skin retraction
- If FNA or core needle shows macrophage fat-laden cells or foreign-body giant cells, it's a benign disease.

- Most masses that contain fat are benign (ex. post-traumatic fat cyst, hamartomas, lipoadenomas).

- There are some malignant tumors that have a benign appearance (smooth, rounded). These include Mucinous Ca, Medullary Ca, and Cystosarcoma Phyllodes.

- **Cystosarcoma Phyllodes** is **malignant** 10% of the time.
- There are no nodes positive, since it has hematogenous spread.
- It can be large, and on pathology it resembles giant fibroadenomas.
- Treatment is a wide local excision. No axillary dissection is required because there is no lymphatic spread.

- "**Stewart-Treves Syndrome**" is lymphangiosarcoma from long-standing lymphedema.
- It can present with dark/purple lesions on the arm, up to 5-10 years after an axillary dissection.

- Mammography and U/S don't work well **during pregnancy**, because the breast tissue becomes dense. If it is required however, do an U/S as opposed to a mammography, to limit radiation.
- If the breast lesion is a cyst, drain it, plus FNA for cytology.
- If the breast lesion is a solid mass, do an FNA or core-needle. If it doesn't help, need an excisional biopsy.
- Breast Ca in pregnancy during any trimester is treated with a mastectomy. If it's late in the 3rd trimester, can do a lumpectomy with axillary node dissection, and radiation after delivery.

THORACIC

- The **thoracic duct** crosses the midline at T4-5, and then drains into the left subclavian vein at its junction with the internal jugular vein.

- The phrenic nerve runs anterior to the pulmonary hilum, whereas the vagus nerve runs posterior.

- **Type 1 pneumocytes** are involved in gas exchange.
- **Type 2 pneumocytes** produce surfactant.

- "**Pores of Kahn**" are pores between adjacent alveoli that allow direct air exchange between alveoli.

- The parietal pleura produces ~1-2 L of fluid per day, which is cleared by the lymphatics.

- The **MC** complications after lobectomy/pneumonectomy are atelectasis and arrhythmias.

- **Lung abscesses** are most commonly associated with aspiration.
- Antibiotics are successful most of the time, but drainage is required if antibiotic therapy fails.

- **Empyema** is usually secondary to pneumonia, though it can also result after any thoracic surgery.
- The exudative and fibroproliferative phase can be treated with a chest tube and antibiotics.
- The organized phase (3 weeks or later) often needs decortication. If it's chronically unresolving, can do an "**Eloesser flap**" (open the chest wall to the outside).

- **Chylothorax** will stain with Sudan Red stain, due to its fatty content.
- This lymphatic fluid is resistant to infection.
- It occurs due to trauma, iatrogenic injury, or due to tumor (lymphoma **MC**, due to its effect on the lymphatics)
- Any insult to the thoracic duct below the midline crossing of the thoracic duct (>T5), will result in a right-sided chylothorax. Above the midline crossing, it causes a left-sided chylothorax.
- Treatment is initially conservative, with a chest tube and low-fat diet. If this fails, need to ligate the thoracic duct very low in the chest (unless it was due to tumor, in which case treat/resect the tumor)

- **Massive hemoptysis** is due to bleeding from bronchial arteries, and is **MCly** secondary to infection (mycetoma being the **MC**).
- **MCC** of death in massive hemoptysis is asphyxiation from the blood in the lungs.
- Treat with a rigid bronchoscopy to identify the side the bleed is from, and then intubate the contralateral lung. If this fails or the patient is unstable, need to do a lobectomy.
- Small hemoptysis can be due to AVM's between pulmonary arteries and veins.

- Treatment of a small primary **spontaneous pneumothorax** in a stable patient is observation.
- A large pneumothorax or a pneumothorax in an unstable patient requires a chest tube.
- If it recurs, continues to have air leak for more than a week, or the lungs don't re-expand after chest tube placement, need surgery.
- Pulmonary blebs need to be resected if a patient is exposed to high-pressure environments (ex. pilots, scuba divers, and mountain climbers).

- **Osteochondromas** are the **MC benign** chest wall tumor.
- **Chondrosarcomas** are the **MC malignant** chest wall tumor.

- Whiteout on CXR with mediastinal shift towards the whiteout is most likely collapse. Treat with a bronchoscopy to remove the obstruction.
- Whiteout on CXR with mediastinal shift away from the whiteout is most likely effusion. Treat by placing a chest tube.

- Continued **hemothorax** despite 2 good chest tubes requires surgical drainage.
- Clotted hemothorax that involves >25% of the lung, or with signs of infection, requires surgical drainage.

Trachea:
- **MC** early complication post-tracheal surgery is edema. Treat by re-intubating, steroids, and racemic epinephrine.
- **MC** late complication post-tracheal surgery is granulation tissue formation.

- **Tracheostomies** need to be between the 1st and 2nd tracheal rings. Any lower and it increases the risk of forming **tracheoinnominate fistulas**.
- Treat tracheoinnominate fistulas by resecting the innominate vessel and using a new tracheostomy site. If there is a lot of bleeding, put a finger in the tracheostomy and hold pressure.

- Treat **tracheoesophageal fistulas** by resecting the fistula, and putting a sternohyoid flap between the trachea and the esophagus.

- **Benign** tumors of the trachea include papillomas and hemangiomas.
- **Malignant** tumors of the trachea include SCC.

Lung Cancer:
- Patients with lung cancer can be asymptomatic.
- It is the **MCC** of cancer-related death in the U.S.
- **AdenoCa** is the MC type of lung cancer.
- Recurrence after resection is usually in the form of metastases. Brain is the **MC** site of metastases.
- Lung Ca has a low 5-year survival, even with resection.

- Diagnosis should begin with a CXR, followed by a CT scan (include the abdomen to look at the adrenals and the liver), sputum cytology, and bronchoscopy with biopsy.
- With bone or brain/neurological symptoms, consider doing a bone scan and a head CT scan to look for metastases.
- With hilar node involvement, consider a **mediastinoscopy** or a "**Chamberlain procedure**" (left 2nd intercostal approach, looks at the anterior mediastinum).

- Of the non-small cell cancers, AdenoCa is more peripheral, SCC is more central.
- Small cell Ca is usually unresectable at the time of diagnosis, and is therefore usually just treated with chemo and radiation.

- **SCC** commonly secretes PTH-related peptide.
- **Small cell Ca** commonly secretes ACTH (it is the **MCC** of paraneoplastic syndrome) and/or ADH.

- **Mesothelioma** is the most **malignant** and aggressive of the lung cancers.

- With a pulmonary coin lesion on a CXR, ~10% are **malignant**, and this risk of malignancy increases with age.
- Generally speaking, slow-growing and a smooth contour suggest benign disease.

- If mediastinal nodes are positive, or there are distant metastases, resection of the lung tumor is not curative.
- Signs that the lung Ca is inoperable include: bloody pleural effusion, Horner's syndrome, vocal cord paralysis, phrenic nerve paralysis, and SVC syndome.

- **Malignant bronchial adenomas** include adenoid cystic adenoma, mucoepidermoid adenoma, and mucous gland adenoma.
- These are slow growing, and spread locally, but do not metastasize.

- **Hamartomas** are the **MC benign** adult lung tumor.
- These have calcifications and can appear as popcorn lesions on a chest CT scan.
- These don't require resection since they are benign, but require repeat CT scans to confirm the diagnosis.

Mediastinal tumors:

- **Neurogenic tumors** are the **overall MC** mediastinal tumors in adults and kids.

- **Anterior mediastinal tumors** include the four T's: **thymus, Thyroid Ca, T-cell lymphoma, Teratoma**.

- **Thymomas** are the **MC anterior mediastinal mass**.
- All thymomas require resection.
- Half of these are **malignant**, half are symptomatic, and half are associated with **Myasthenia-Gravis** (M-G).
- Most M-G patients (even those that don't have a thymoma) will improve with a thymectomy.

- With **mediastinal lymphomas**, non-Hodgkin's T-cell lymphomas are the **MC** type.
- Within the Hodgkin's types, nodular sclerosing is the **MC** type.
- Treat lymphomas with chemo and radiation.

- **Mediastinal germ cell tumors** need a mediastinoscopic biopsy.
- **Teratomas** are overall the **MC** of these mediastinal germ cell tumors. Treat with resection and chemo.
- **Seminomas** are the **MC malignant** mediastinal germ cell tumor. Treat with radiation and chemo.
- **Non-seminomas** have elevated β-hCG and α-FP. Treat these with radiation and chemo.

- **Bronchogenic cysts** are the **MC** type of mediastinal cyst.

CARDIAC

- Right to left shunting in the heart causes cyanosis, whereas left to right shunting causes CHF symptoms. In kids, hepatomegaly is the first sign of CHF.
- **"Eisenmenger's syndrome"** is when a left to right shift turns into a right to left shift due to increased pulmonary vascular resistance.

Left to Right shunting:

- **VSD** is the **overall MC congenital** heart defect.
- Symptoms start at ~4-6 weeks: as the pulmonary vascular resistance goes down, it increases the left to right shunt.
- Most of these close spontaneously by 6 months.
- Since this is left to right shunting, we get CHF symptoms. Treatment is therefore diuretics and digoxin.
- Surgery is needed if there is failure to thrive or if it does not resolve spontaneously by school age.

- **ASD** is **MCly** caused by an Ostium Secundum defect, resulting in a patent foramen ovale.
- Since this is also left to right shunting, symptoms are also CHF symptoms, and hence treatment is again diuretics and digoxin.
- Surgery is required if it doesn't close spontaneously by school age (just like VSD), or if it's an Ostium Primum defect.
- ASD is sometimes associated with anomalous pulmonary venous return, where the pulmonary vein drains into the SVC instead of draining in the left atrium.

Right to Left shunting:

- **Tetralogy of Fallot** is the **MC** of the cyanotic (right to left) congenital heart defects.
- Initial treatment consists of β-blockade.
- Surgery is eventually required, but can delay a definitive repair until later in childhood by using a **"Blalock-Taussig shunt"**, which is a shunt between the subclavian artery and the ipsilateral pulmonary artery.

- **Transposition of the great vessels** is the **MC** cyanotic congential heart defect to present in the 1st week of life.
- Treatment includes giving PGE2, which is not only a bronchodilator, but also a vasodilator, so it will keep the ductus arteriosum patent.
- As with Tetralogy of Fallot, can delay a definitive repair with a **Blalock-Taussig shunt**.

- **Truncus Arteriosus** is when there's no septum dividing the pulmonary artery and the aorta.
- These are usually associated with a VSD.
- Even though this is right to left shunting, neonates with this often present with CHF symptoms, and most will die in their 1st year of life due to this CHF.

Other congenital anomalies:

- **Patent Ductus Arteriosus** (PDA) can be closed using indomethacin (in order to decrease prostaglandin production), though this only works in the neonatal period.
- If the PDA persists beyond this period, a left thoracotomy is required to repair it.

- **Coarctation of the aorta** is usually just distal to the left subclavian artery, and is associated with Turner's syndrome.
- Surgical repair is indicated to prevent heart failure.

- A **univentricular heart** requires a "**Fontan procedure**", which involves diverting venous blood from the right atrium directly to the pulmonary arteries (by-passing the ventricle).

- A **hypoplastic left heart** is treated with a "**Norwood procedure**" in which:
- All incoming venous blood (both systemic and pulmonary) drains into the right atrium.
- The right ventricle is connected to the ascending aorta instead of the pulmonary artery. The right ventricle therefore supplies blood to the systemic circulation.
- The pulmonary arteries receive blood from a **Blalock-Taussig shunt**.

- "**Vascular rings**" are congenital anomalies resulting in the encircling of structures by the aortic arch and/or great vessels.
- A double aortic arch is the **MC** type of these "vascular rings". This wraps around the esophagus and trachea, and therefore can present with dysphagia and/or pulmonary infections.
- Treatment is to ligate the smaller of the two arches.

Miscellaneous:

- **CAD** is the **MCC of death** in the U.S.

- Most of the population is said to be "**right dominant**": the posterior descending artery comes off the Right coronary artery.
- The Left coronary artery splits to give the Left anterior descending artery (LAD) and the Circumflex artery.

- Free wall rupture post-MI is **MC** 3-7 days post-MI.
- VSD post-MI is **MC** 5-7 days post-MI.

- Internal mammary arteries are the best conduits for use in CABG (better than saphenous veins).
- During CABG, the heart is arrested using K^+ and cold solution.
- Indications for CABG include left main disease, 3 vessel disease, or 2 vessel disease with LAD stenosis.
- Emergency CABG is the biggest risk factor for mortality.

- **Rheumatic heart disease** is the **MCC** of valve disease in the U.S., and it **MCly** affects the mitral valve.
- Surgery for valve disease in RHD is usually reserved for symptomatic cases.

- **Endocarditis MCly** affects the mitral valve, unless the patient has prosthetic valves, in which case it **MCly** affects the aortic valve.
- In intravenous drug abusers, endocarditis **MCly** affects the tricuspid valve.
- Initial treatment is with antibiotics.
- Indications for surgery include failure of antibiotics, valve failure, pericarditis, or perivalvular abscesses.

- Tissue valves are not as durable as mechanical valves, and so avoid them in younger patients.

- Prosthetic valves, RHD, congenital heart defects, and mitral valve prolapse all require procedural antibiotics for endocarditis prophylaxis.

- **Myxomas** are the **MC benign** tumors of the heart. Most are in the left atrium.
- **Angiosarcomas** are the **MC malignant** tumor of the heart.
- **Lung Ca** is the **MC** metastatic tumor of the heart.

- Coronary veins have the lowest O_2 content, due to the myocardium's high O_2 extraction.

- Mediastinal bleeding >500 cc over the first hour post cardiac surgery is an indication to re-explore.

- First sign of cardiac tamponade on echo is decreased passive filling of the atria.

VASCULAR

- **MC congenital** hypercoagulable disorder is Factor 5 Leiden (CF5 resistant to deactivation by Protein C).
- **MC acquired** hypercoagulable disorder is smoking.

- **Atherosclerosis** begins with foam cells (macrophages that absorbed fat/lipids in vessel walls), that release GF's resulting in smooth muscle proliferation.
- This smooth muscle proliferation results in vessel wall injury and intimal disruption, resulting in collagen exposure in the vessel wall which promotes thrombus formation.
- Thrombi eventually become fibrous plaques as a result of calcifications/necrosis/hemorrhage.

- Atherosclerosis is a disease of the intima, whereas HTN is a disease of the media.

Cerebrovascular disease:

- Stroke is the 3rd **MCC** of death in U.S.
- HTN is the biggest risk factor for stroke.
- Ischemic strokes are **MCly** due to emboli, and not thrombosis.
- **MC** source of embolus in strokes is from the internal carotid arteries. The 2nd **MC** source of embolus is from the heart.
- The middle cerebral artery is the **MCly** diseased intracranial artery.

- Vertebral artery diseases are usually bilateral at the time of diagnosis, because needs to be bilateral to have symptoms.
- Symptoms include diplopia, dysarthria, vertigo, tinnitus, and incoordination.
- Treatment can be either percutaneous angioplasty, surgical resection of the musculotendinous bands, or vertebral artery transposition to the subclavian artery.

Carotid disease:

- **Carotid arteries** provide 85% of the brain's blood supply.
- A normal internal carotid artery has continuous flow. A normal external carotid artery has triphasic flow.

- The first branch off the external carotid artery is the superior thyroid artery.

- There is a communication between the internal and external carotids via the ophthalmic and internal maxillary arteries.

- Amaurosis Fugax is occlusion of the ophthalmic branch of the internal carotid artery (on ophthalmic exam, see "**Hollenhorst plaques**").

- The carotid bifurcation is the **MC** site of stenosis (due to the turbulent flow).

- **Carotid endarterectomy** is indicated if there is >80% stenosis, or >70% with symptoms.
- If there has been a recent stroke, wait 4-6 weeks before doing an endarterectomy.
- Emergent endarterectomy can be considered if there are fluctuating neurologic symptoms or evolving TIA's.
- During an endarterectomy we need a shunt if the distal stump pressure is <50.

- If there is bilateral carotid disease, than repair the worst side first (the right side is usually the worst side).

- **MC** nerve injury complication during an endarterectomy is a CN 10 injury (causing voice hoarseness).
- Can also damage CN 12 and the mandibular branch of CN 7.
- If a patient gets an acute cerebral event shortly after an endarterectomy, need to bring the patient back to the OR to check for a thrombosis, or for an occluding intimal flap.
- Pulsatile/bleeding mass status post endarterectomy, think **Pseudoaneurysm**.
- It's common to get HTN after an endarterectomy due to the manipulation of the carotid body.
- **MCC** of morbidity/mortality status post endarterectomy is a stroke. MI is the **MC non-stroke** morbidity/mortality.
- ~15% of endarterectomies re-stenose.

- Carotid stenting is an alternative treatment for carotid disease. It is most beneficial for those at high-risk for surgery (ex. >80 years old, MI in last 4 weeks, EF <30%, on dialysis, severe COPD).

- **Carotid body tumors** are **MCly** neural crest in origin.

Thoracic aortic disease:

- **Transections** are usually a result of trauma (deceleration injury). They are not commonly encountered, since 90% die at the scene.
- Tears are **MC** at the ligamentum arteriosum (just distal to left subclavian).
- The mediastinal widening seen here is a result of tears from bridging arteries/veins, and not from the aorta.
- When repairing these, need a left heart bypass.

- **Aneurysms** in the ascending aorta are usually caused by Connective Tissue disorders causing cystic medial necrosis (i.e. Marfan's or Ehlers-Danlos).
- They are often asymptomatic and accidentally picked up on a CXR, but can cause vertebral compression (back pain), recurrent laryngeal nerve pressure (voice change), pressure on the bronchi (dyspnea), pressure on the esophagus (dysphagia), or CHF due to aortic regurge.
- Avoid angiograms in Ehlers-Danlos because they have a tendency for arterial rupture, which are hard to repair due to the weak connective tissue, and often require ligation.

- Aneurysms in the aortic arch are usually caused by atherosclerosis.

- Aneurysms in the descending/thoracic aorta are also usually caused by atherosclerosis.
- They carry a 5-10% risk of paraplegia due to damage to arteries supplying the vertebrae.

- Treatment for all thoracic aneurysms is required if they become acutely symptomatic, rapidly increase in size, or if they are >7cm (or >6cm in Marfan's).

- In **thoracic aortic dissections**: Type 1 involves both the ascending and descending aorta, Type 2 involves the ascending aorta, Type 3 involves the descending aorta.
- Dissections occur in the medial layer of the aorta.
- Symptoms can mimic those of an MI, or can have tearing chest pain or unequal BP/pulses in the upper extremities.
- Can get an MI here if the dissection is in the ascending aorta and occludes the coronaries.
- In ascending aortic dissections, death is usually due to cardiac failure from regurge or tamponade.
- Treatment is initially BP control. All ascending aortic dissections eventually will need surgical repair due to risk of death from regurge or tamponade. Descending aortic dissections need surgical repair if there is visceral, renal or leg ischemia.
- Patients with thoracic aortic dissection need lifetime CT's, since many will develop aneurysms.

- A surgical complication specific to thoracic aortic surgeries is paraplegia.

- This is due to occlusion of the intercostals and/or the artery of Adamkiewicz (Anterior Segmental Medullary artery), which supplies blood to the lower 2/3 of the anterior spinal artery.
- To prevent this, re-implant the intercostals below T8 to maintain flow to the intercostals.

Abdominal aortic disease:

- **Abdominal aortic aneurysms** (AAA's) are caused by degeneration of the medial layer, and are **MCly** due to atherosclerosis.

- Risk of rupture for an AAA starts at 5cm, with a 15-20% risk of rupture in 5 years.
- **MC** site for an AAA rupture is the posterolateral walls, 2-4 cm below the renals.
- The biggest risk factors for rupture are diastolic HTN and COPD.
- Even if a patient with rupture makes it to hospital, there's a 50% risk of mortality.

- In about 10% of AAA's, we get inflammation leading to adhesions.

- Aneurysms can develop due to infection, if bacteria infect atherosclerotic plaques.
- The **MC** organism involved in aneurysms is Salmonella, and blood cultures are often negative.

- When repairing AAA's, need to reimplant the IMA if the backbleeding pressure is <40, or if there's been previous colonic surgery (because it will affect the anastomoses between SMA-IMA and internal iliac-IMA.

- Lumbar arteries in the abdomen can be ligated (unlike in the thorax).

- **MCC** of acute death status post AAA repair is MI.
- **MCC** of late death status post AAA repair is renal failure.
- **MCC** non-fatal complication is atherosclerotic occlusion.

- With diarrhea status post AAA repair, think ischemic colitis. Can check this with a colonoscopy or a CT scan (sigmoidoscopy will not suffice, because the rectum is spared due to its blood supply off the internal iliacs).
- If peritoneal signs are present as well, take the patient to the OR. Otherwise just follow.

- With graft infections, blood cultures are often negative. Treatment is to resect the graft and to bypass the area, thereby avoiding the contaminated graft and surrounding tissue. This is done with an axillary-femoral bypass.

- Aortoenteric fistulas can develop after an AAA repair. They **MCly** involve the 3rd/4th portions of the duodenum, and **MCly** occur ~6 months after surgery.
- Symptoms include hematemesis, blood per rectum, and "herald bleed" (small GI bleed before a full-blown bleed).
- Treatment is an axillary-fem bypass, and closing the Aorta.

- Endovascular stented tube grafts are typically reserved for AAA's <7cm.
- Complications of endovascular AAA repairs include leaks: a Type 1 endoleak is either at the proximal or distal end of the graft. A type 2 endoleak is backbleeding from the lumbar arteries or the IMA into the aneurysm sac. Type 3 endoleak is due to graft tears/disconnection/disintegration. Type 4 endoleak is through the stent.

Lower Extremity vascular disease:

- The lower leg has 4 compartments: **anterior**, **lateral**, **superficial**, and **deep posterior**.
- Anterior contains the deep peroneal nerve (which provides sensation between 1st & 2nd toes).
- Lateral contains the superficial peroneal nerve.
- Superficial contains the sural nerve.
- Deep contains the tibial nerve.

- Statins are the main preventative agents against atherosclerosis.

- **Homocysteinuria** can promote atherosclerosis.
- Treatment is Vitamin B12 and Folate to drive the Methionine synthase reaction towards Methionine, thereby using up Homocysteine.

- **Claudication** has a 2% per year risk of gangrene.
- Symptoms of claudication can also be from Lumbar stenosis or Diabetic neuropathy (numbness, weakness, rest pains).

- "**Leriche syndrome**" is a lesion at the aortic bifurcation or above, causing butt/thigh claudication, impotence, and weak femoral pulses.

- The **MC** location for an atherosclerotic occlusion in the lower extremities is in **Hunter's/Adductor canal** in the superior portion of the femoral triangle.
- The femoral triangle is bordered by the inguinal ligament, Sartorius muscle, and adductor longus muscle.

- ABI <0.6 results in rest pains. <0.5 typically results in the formation of ulcers. <0.3 often results in gangrene.
- ABI's are not accurate in diabetics.

- Below knee femoral-popliteal bypass has the best outcome using a vein graft.
- For an above knee femoral-popliteal bypass, can use a synthetic graft.

- Post-operative swelling after a lower extremity vascular case could be either a DVT or reperfusion injury.
- In **reperfusion injury**, look for lactic acidosis, hyperkalemia, myoglobinuria, and compartment syndrome.
- **MC** compartment affected in **compartment syndrome** is the anterior compartment, which contains the deep peroneal nerve. A pressure of >20-30 mmHg is abnormal, although diagnosis is clinical.

- With a reversed saphenous vein graft, a surgical/technical complication is the **MCC** of early failure. Atherosclerosis is the **MCC** of late failure.

- Patients with ulcerations to the bone typically need an amputation.
- Wet gangrene is a surgical emergency.

- A "**Malperforans ulcer**" is an ulcer of the metatarsal heads (**MCly** affected is the 2nd MTP joint).
- Treatment involves no weight bearing, debridement, antibiotics, and possibly revascularization.

- "**Popliteal entrapment syndrome**" is caused by medial deviation of the Popliteal artery around the medial head of the gastrocnemius muscle.
- It presents with loss of pedal pulses with plantarflexion.
- Treatment is resection of the medial head of the gastrocnemius muscle.

- "**Adventitial Cystic disease**" **MCly** affects the popliteal artery, and causes intermittent claudication that changes with knee flexion/extension.
- Treatment is resection of the cysts. If the vessel is occluded, then treat it like any other lower extremity occlusion (vein graft, etc).

- Amputations (above or below knee) have a 50% mortality rate within 3 years.

- **MC** site of a lower extremity obstruction from an arterial embolus is the Common femoral artery, with **MC** source being from the heart (A. Fib).

- Permanent muscle and nerve damage with ischemia begins at 4-6 hours.
- If a patient therefore presents >4-6 hours post-ischemia, need to do a fasciotomy.

- In thrombosis, it's usually a chronic problem, it's usually bilateral, and there are therefore often collaterals.
- With emboli we don't have collaterals, because it's not a chronic problem.

- If a limb is threatened (ex. pulseless with sensory deficits), treatment is an urgent embolectomy/thrombectomy.
- If a limb is ischemic but not threatened (no sensory deficits), thrombolysis can be attempted.
- For **thrombolytic therapy** to work, a guide-wire has to be able to get past the obstruction.
- Contraindications to thrombolytic therapy include pregnancy, presence of a heart thrombus, recent surgery, aortic dissection, active bleeding, pericarditis, and history of recent TIA's/strokes.

Renal vascular disease:

- The right renal artery runs behind the IVC, and there are accessory renal arteries in 25% of the population.

- Most renal emboli are from the heart.

- Diastolic BP of >115 might be indicative of a renal vascular etiology.

- **Renal atherosclerosis** is **MC** in the left renal artery, in the proximal 1/3 of the renal artery, and in men.
- **Fibromuscular dysplasia** on the other hand is **MC** on the right renal artery, in distal 1/3 of the renal artery, and in women. This has a "string of beads" appearance and can also involve the carotids and iliacs.
- Treatment for both is stenting.

- Surgery for the treatment of renal artery stenosis in the form of recanalization can be considered if there is a simultaneous AAA, a renal artery aneurysm, or failed angioplasty/stenting.

Upper extremity:

- Occlusive diseases of the upper extremity usually involve the subclavian artery, but are often asymptomatic due to collaterals.

- In "**Subclavian steal syndrome**", the distal subclavian 'steals' blood from the vertebral artery (via reversed flow) due to a proximal subclavian artery stenosis.
- Treat this only if the reversal of blood flow from the vertebral artery causes neurological symptoms.

- Both the subclavian artery and vein pass over the 1st rib.
- Subclavian vein passes anterior to the anterior scalene.
- Subclavian artery (along with the brachial plexus) passes between the anterior and middle scalenes (in the so-called "thoracic outlet").

- In **Thoracic outlet syndrome**, the subclavian artery and brachial plexus get compressed in the

Thoracic outlet.
- "**Adson's test**" is a decrease in the radial pulse when the head is turned to the ipsilateral side, and is indicative of Thoracic outlet syndrome.
- **MCC** of thoracic outlet syndrome is a cervical rib, and the **MCC** of pain is due to brachial plexus irritation.
- The subclavian artery can also get compressed by hypertrophy of the anterior scalene muscle, like in pitchers.
- Here the radial pulse diminishes with maximal arm abduction.

- "**Paget-Von Schrötter disease**" is thrombosis of the subclavian/axillary vein. It presents with pain and swelling that worsens with activity (hence so-called "effort-induced") and gets better with rest.

Mesenteric ischemia:
- Mesenteric ischemia has an overall mortality rate of 50-70%.

- CT scan findings include bowel wall thickening, intramural gas, portal vein gas, and vascular occlusion.

- **MCC** of mesenteric ischemia is emboli from the heart, followed by a thrombus and low-flow state (ex. shock).

- With an SMA thrombosis, symptoms are usually chronic, like food fear.

- A bruit near the epigastrium is indicative of "**Median Arcuate Ligament syndrome**".
- In this syndrome, the ligament that connects the right and left crura of the diaphragm (the Median Arcuate ligament) causes celiac artery compression.

Non-Aortic Aneurysms:
- Symptomatic, mycotic, or visceral (except Splenic) aneurysms all require repair.

- Above the inguinal ligament, the **MC** complication of aneurysms is rupture.
- Below the inguinal ligament, thrombosis and emboli are the **MC** complications of aneurysms.

- All **visceral aneurysms** require surgical repair except for Splenic artery aneurysms, which are the **MC** type of visceral aneurysm, yet carry the lowest risk of rupture.
- Splenic artery aneurysms only require repair if they are symptomatic, or in pregnant women/women of child-bearing age because of the high risk of rupture during pregnancy (usually in 3rd trimester when the uterus is high enough to put pressure on the spleen).

- **Splenic and common hepatic artery aneurysms** can be treated with exclusion (instead of bypass), since they have good collaterals.
- Visceral aneurysms can develop due to local inflammation (ex. pancreatitis), or portal HTN.

- **Renal aneurysms** need repair if they are >1.5cm or in pregnant women/women of child-bearing age, due to the risk of rupture. These may require a nephrectomy if the renal artery aneurysm ruptures.

- **Iliac and Femoral artery aneurysms** need repair if they are >2.5cm.
- Popliteal artery is the **MC** type of peripheral aneurysm. Half the time it's bilateral, and half the time there is another aneurysm elsewhere.
- Since the **MC** complication of aneurysms below the inguinal ligament is thrombosis/embolism, these typically present with limb ischemia.
- Treatment of Popliteal aneurysms is indicated if they are >2cm. If left untreated, almost 25% will have complications that will require an amputation.

- A **pseudoaneurysm** is a collection of blood in continuity of the artery, but contained within all layers of the arterial wall. It can develop after any arteriography.
- Diagnosis is with a duplex U/S, and treatment is with U/S-guided thrombin injection.
- If it is due to a disruption of a graft-artery anastomosis site, treatment is surgical.

Other vascular diseases:
- **Buerger's disease** is seen in smokers. It presents with severe distal, bilateral, disease (gangrene of digits) and rest pains. Everything proximal however is usually normal. Smoking cessation often cures it.

- **Temporal arteritis** affects the temporal artery and can present with headaches and visual disturbances. It can also affect branches off the aorta or the aorta itself, as well as pulmonary arteries.
- The visual disturbances are due to inflammation of the temporal arteries.
- Patients affected are typically women >35 years old.
- Treatment is steroids.

- **Takayasu's arteritis** can have same symptoms similar to those of Temporal Arteritis, and treatment is the same, but it usually affects young Asian women <35 years old.

- **Polyarteritis Nodosa** affects the kidneys and the GI.
- Perinuclear staining anti-neutrophil cytoplasmic antibodies (p-ANCA) are seen here. Treatment is steroids.

- **Kawasaki's disease** affects children. It can affect the coronary arteries and can therefore cause fatal arrhythmias.
- Treatment is IV Immunoglobulin and Aspirin.

- **Hypersensitivity angitis** is typically due to drugs, and treatment is vasodilation (Ca^+-channel blockers or Pentoxifylline (a PDE4-blocker)).

- **Radiation arteritis** initially causes sloughing and thrombosis. Over time, it's more likely to present with scarring and stenosis.

Venous diseases:
- **MCC** of an arteriovenous graft failure is venous obstruction due to intimal hyperplasia.

- In a young, otherwise healthy patient who presents with CHF symptoms, consider an arteriovenous fistula somewhere.

- A DVT is a contraindication for varicose vein stripping.

- **Thrombophlebitis** can be infectious or non-infectious.
- Infectious/suppurative thrombophlebitis will present with fever, increased WBC and needs to be treated with vein resection. Otherwise can just treat with NSAIDs and warm packs.

- Migrating thrombophlebitis can be a sign of pancreatic Ca.

- "**Mondor's disease**" is self-limiting thrombophlebitis of superficial veins of the breast and anterior chest.

- "**May-Thurner syndrome**" is DVT in the left lower extremities due to compression of the left common iliac vein by the overlying left common iliac artery.

- "**Phlegmasia Alba Dolens**" is when only the deep venous channels are affected (white).
- "**Phlegmasia Cerulea Dolens**" is when the collaterals are affected as well. This therefore causes more massive edema (blue).

- First-time **DVT** is treated with Coumadin for 6 months. A second DVT warrants Coumadin therapy for one year. A third DVT or a PE requires lifetime Coumadin therapy.
- If a patient can't take anticoagulation medication (ex. active bleeding), or develops a PE while taking Coumadin, then an IVC filter is required.
- A PE in a patient with an IVC filter indicates that the embolus may from a location other than the lower extremities, such as from the ovarian veins or from an upper extremity vein.

- If a pulmonary embolus patient is in shock, consider going to the OR for an emergency embolectomy.

Lymphatics:

- Lymphatics do not contain a basement membrane, and are not found in the brain, muscle, bone/tendon/cartilage, or cornea.

- Treatment of lymphedema is limb elevation, compression, and antibiotics if suspecting an infection as the cause.

- Lymphangiosarcoma is a **malignant** tumor of the lymphatics, often occurring as a result of long-standing lymphedema.
- It usually presents with raised purple discoloration of the skin or tender skin nodules, eventually progressing to necrosis. It metastasizes quickly, **MCly** to the lungs.
- When this follows axillary dissection (like in a mastectomy, causing long-standing lymphedema), it's called "**Stewart-Treves syndrome**". It can occur up to 5-10 years status post axillary dissection.

- **Lymphoceles** are lymph containing sacs, which typically arise from injured lymphatic channels (ex. following surgery).
- These are common after groin dissections.
- Need to first rule out an infectious cause for the drainage; send fluid for culture/analysis.
- Small lymphoceles can be observed, because they might get reabsorbed.
- Large/symptomatic lymphoceles, or lymphoceles close to graft material, require early excision.
- Before excising, inject Isosulfan blue dye into the limb to identify the lymphatic channels that supply the lymphocele. Then resect the lymphocele and ligate the supplying channels.

UROLOGY

- The right renal artery passes posterior to the IVC
- The ureters travel posterior to the gonadal arteries, but anterior the iliac arteries.
- The left gonadal vein drains into the left renal vein.

- Sperm production occurs in the seminiferous tubules. Sperm then travels to the rete testis, followed by the epididymis, before going to the vas deferens.

- Hypotension is the **MCC** of acute renal insufficiency following surgery.

Kidney stones:

- **Calcium Oxalate** stones are the **MC** type of kidney stone.
- The risk of Calcium Oxalate stone formation increases with terminal ileum resections, as a result of increased oxalate absorption and decreased Calcium absorption. (The reason is because too much bile gets into the colon, increasing the permeability to oxalate, but also bile binding to Calcium and decreasing Calcium absorption)

- **Struvite stones** are due to protease producing bacteria (ex. Proteus).

- **Uric acid** stones are radiolucent.

Testicular cancers:

- Testicular cancer is the main cancer killer in young men.

- With any testicular cancer, need an orchiectomy through an inguinal incision (not a transscrotal incision).

- Most testicular masses are **malignant**. So do a chest XR/CT and an abdominal CT to look for metastases. And also get β-HCG and AFP levels for baseline.

- LDH levels correlate with tumor bulk.

- Most testicular cancers are Germ cell cancers (seminoma or non-seminoma).

- **Seminomas** are the most-common testicular tumor.
- β-HCG is only sometimes elevated in seminomas, AFP is rarely ever elevated.
- This is extremely sensitive to radiation, so treat all stages of seminomas with an orchiectomy and retroperitoneal radiation.
- If there are positive nodes or metastatic disease, add chemo as well.
- If the paraaortic nodes are enlarged, extend the radiation to the mediastinum.

- **Nonseminomatous** testicular cancers can be embryonal Ca, chorioCa, or yolk sac Ca.
- Both β-HCG and AFP are elevated here.
- Apart from retroperitoneal spread, these also spread hematogenously to the lungs.
- Treatment is orchiectomy and retroperitoneal node dissection. If it's stage 2 (spread to retroperitoneal lymph nodes), need chemo / radiation as well.

Prostate cancer:

- The posterior lobe of the prostate is the **MC** site for prostate Ca, and bone is the **MC** site of metastases.
- For intracapsular tumors with no metastases (T1or T2), treat with a radical prostatectomy, radiation, and pelvic lymph node dissection.
- For extracapsular or metastatic disease, treat with hormones, bilateral orchiectomy, and radiation.
- With a prostatectomy, PSA should get close to 0 after 3 weeks. Otherwise get a bone scan to check for metastases.
- PSA can also be increased by prostatitis, BPH, and chronic catheterization.

Renal Cell Ca (RCC):

- **RCC** is the **MC primary** tumor of the kidneys. (The **overall MC** tumor of kidneys is metastases from the breast)
- Smoking is a risk factor.
- Pain, mass, and hematuria is the classic triad seen in RCC (+/- erythrocytosis).
- RCC can be seen as part of "**Von-Hippel Lindau syndrome**", which is RCC, renal cysts, CNS tumors, and pheochromocytoma.
- About a third of patients presenting with RCC have metastases by the time of diagnosis; lungs being the **MC** site for metastases.
- Treatment is a Radical nephrectomy (removing the adrenals, surrounding fat, Gerota's fascia, and nodes), as well as chemo / radiation.
- If it grows into the IVC, can still resect it; simply pull the tumor thrombus out of the IVC.
- If the tumor involves the ureter, likely to be Transitional Cell Ca, and not RCC. Treatment is the same, but also need to resect the ureter.

- A kidney mass can also be an angiomyolipoma or a hamartoma. Treat these if they are >4cm.

Bladder Ca:

- Other than smoking, aniline dyes and cyclophosphamide are also risk factors.
- If it's T1 (muscle not involved), can do a transurethral resection.
- If muscle is involved (T2 or higher), need a cystectomy with an ileal conduit, as well as chemo / radiation.
- With SCC of the bladder, look for Schistosomiasis.
- An ileal conduit predisposes to kidney stones, because the segment of ileum used in the conduit will reabsorb urinary Calcium.

Incontinence:

- **Stress incontinence** is due to loss of sphincter control/strength
- Treatment is Kegel exercises, or a sling.

- **Urge incontinence** is due to involuntary detrusor contractions.
- Treatment is anticholinergics, and behavior modifications.

- **Overflow incontinence** is due to incomplete emptying, and hence overflow and leakage.
- Treatment is TURP since it's often due to BPH.

- **Congenital incontinence** presents with continuous leakage due to a bypassed sphincter mechanism.

Benign Prostatic Hyperplasia (BPH):

- **BPH** arises from the transitional zone of the prostate.
- Initial therapy consists of an α-1 receptor blocker (ex. Prazosin or Tamsulosin), and a 5-α reductase inhibitor (ex. finasteride).
- A transurethral resection of the prostate (TURP) is indicated for failure of medical therapy. "**Post-TURP syndrome**" includes hyponatremia, seizures, and cerebral edema due to the irrigation with water (all that water can get absorbed). Treatment is diuresis.
- TURP can also result in retrograde ejaculation into the bladder.

Miscellaneous:

- Ureteral trauma is treated with a primary repair. Use absorbable suture to avoid stone formation, and stent the ureter to avoid stenosis. Consider placing retroperitoneal drains to be able to assess for anastomotic leaks.

- **Neurogenic bladder** is **MCly** due to a spinal injury above T12, and is due to patients not being able to hold their urine.
- Treatment is surgical, like with a sling.

- **Neurogenic obstructive uropathy** is **MCly** due to a spinal injury below T12, and is due to incomplete emptying.
- Treatment is intermittent catheterization.

- Ureteral duplication is the **MC** congenital urinary tract abnormality.

- Failure of closure of the urachus during embryonal development can leave a connection between the bladder and the umbilicus.

- In **Polycystic Kidney disease** (PKD), resection is only required if it's symptomatic.

- **Epididymitis** is not always infectious. Can get sterile epididymitis simply from straining.

- WBC casts indicate a pyelonephritis or a glomerulonephritis
- RBC casts indicate a glomerulonephritis

- Treatment of **priapism** is aspiration and also Epinephrine or Phenylephrine to constrict the blood vessels carrying blood to the penis. If these fail, may need surgery.

GYNECOLOGY

- **Broad ligament** contains the uterine vessels.
- **Infundibular ligament** contains the ovarian artery, vein, and nerve.
- **Cardinal ligament** holds the cervix and vagina.

- Most pregnancies can be seen on U/S at 6 weeks.

- **Endometriosis** is endometrial tissue outside the endometrial cavity.
- It presents with dysmenorrhea, infertility, and dyspareunia.
- The ovaries are **MCly** affected.
- Can involve the rectum and cause cyclical GI bleeding during menses.
- Treatment is OCP's.

- **Pelvic inflammatory disease** (PID) increases the risk of infertility and ectopic pregnancy.
- Treatment is antibiotics covering both Chlamydia and Neisseria (ex. Cefoxitin and Doxycycline).

- **"Mittelschmerz"** is the term used for mid-menstrual pains, caused by rupture of the Graafian follicle.

- **Vaginal Ca** is **MCly** primary and is usually SCC.
- Treatment is radiation.

- Previous exposure to DES can cause Clear cell Ca of the vagina. This carries a worst prognosis than SCC.

- Vulvar cancers <2cm can be treated with a wide local excision and ipsilateral node dissection.
- Vulvar cancers >2cm require a vulvectomy, bilateral node dissection, and also radiation if margins are <1cm.

Ovarian Ca:

- **Ovarian Ca** is the **MCC** of gynecological death. Unopposed Estrogen (early menses, nulliparity, late menopause) increases the risk.
- Sertoli-Leydig cell tumors are androgen-secreting, hence present with masculinization.
- Granulosa-Theca cell tumors are estrogen-secreting, hence present with precocious puberty.
- Struma Ovarii contains thyroid tissue.
- Stage 1 ovarian Ca is limited to the ovaries. Stage 2 is limited to the pelvis. Stage 3 is below the diaphragm.
- The **MC** initial site of spread of ovarian Ca is the contralateral ovary (this is still considered Stage 1).
- Treatment is TAH/BSO for all stages of ovarian Ca.

- **Krukenberg tumor** is ovarian Ca originating form the GI tract. On Histology, it has characteristic signet ring cells.

- **"Meige's syndrome"** is ascites and hydrothorax due to an ovarian fibroma. Excising the tumor cures the ascites/hydrothorax.

Endometrial Ca:

- **Endometrial Ca** is the **MC malignant** gynecological Ca.

- Risk factors are the same as Ovarian Ca: unopposed Estrogen.
- Stage 1 endometrial Ca is limited to the uterus. Stage 2 involves but is contained within the cervix. Stage 3 involves the vagina or ovaries. Stage 4 is anywhere else (bladder, rectum, etc).
- Treatment for all stages is TAH/BSO (just like Ovarian Ca), but also radiation.

Cervical Ca:

- **Cervical Ca** is **MCly** SCC. It's associated with HPV 16 & 18.
- The obturator nodes are first to be affected.
- Stage 2 involves the upper 1/3 of the vagina. Stage 3 involves the lower vagina and the pelvis. Stage 4 is everywhere else (bladder, rectum, etc).
- Treatment is cone biopsy for cervical Ca in-situ, and TAH for the others. Stage 3 and 4 also require radiation.

Miscellaneous:

- Complete Hydatidiform mole is of paternal origin (empty egg fertilized by a sperm).
- Partial Hydatidiform mole is a normal egg fertilized by two sperms.

NEUROSURGERY

- The vertebral arteries come together to form the Basilar artery, which then branches off into the Posterior cerebral arteries.

- **Microglial cells** are the Macrophages of the CNS: they phagocytose dead tissue, bacteria, etc.

- **Neurapraxia** is the mildest form of nerve injury. It is a transient episode of motor paralysis, with no sensory dysfunction

- Injured nerves regenerate at a rate of 1 mm/day

- ADH is made in the hypothalamus (supraoptic nuclei) but released into the blood by the posterior pituitary.

- Half of cerebral AVM's will present with sudden headache or loss of consciousness. Treatment is to resect the AVM.

- **Subarachnoid hemorrhage** is often caused by a ruptured cerebral aneurysm (cerebral aneurysms are **MC** in the anterior communicating artery).
- Symptoms include severe headache, photophobia, and stiff neck.
- Treatment is aggressive fluid resuscitation and Ca-channel blockers (to prevent vasospasms (and therefore ischemia) to other parts of the brain).
- If stable, do angiographic clipping/coiling. An unstable patient may need surgery to evacuate the blood.

- Treatment for vertebral **disc herniation** is NSAID's, heat, rest, and surgery only for substantial or progressive neurological defects.

- **Spinal shock** as a result of spinal cord injury can cause peripheral vasodilation due to the loss of a sympathetic tone.
- Treatment requires pressors to maintain an adequate blood pressure.

- **Anterior Spinal syndrome** causes bilateral loss of motor, pain, and temperature, but since the dorsal columns are intact, proprioception is unaffected.

- **Brown-Sequard syndrome** (lateral hemisection of the spinal cord) causes ipsilateral loss of motor, and contralateral loss of pain and temperature below level of lesion.

- **Central cord syndrome** (caused by hyperflexion of the cervical spine) causes bilateral loss of motor, pain, and temperature in the upper extremities. (The lower extremities are spared since their nerves travel on the periphery of the spinal cord)

- **Brain cancer** is **MCly** metastatic in origin (**MCly** from the lungs, breast, or skin (melanoma)).
- **Gliomas** are the **MC primary** brain tumors.

- **Medulloblastomas** are the **MC** brain tumors in kids.
- **Neuroblastomas** are the **MC** metastatic brain tumors in kids.

- **Acoustic neuromas** arise from the 8th cranial nerve, and present with hearing loss, vertigo, n/v, and imbalance/ unsteadiness.

- **Myelomeningocele** is herniation of the spinal cord and nerve roots through a vertebral defect.
- If the hernia sac ruptures, need surgery to prevent infection of the spinal cord.

- Premature infants commonly get **intraventricular hemorrhaging**, since they have fragile vessels in their germinal matrix.
- Treatment requires a ventricular catheter to drain the blood and prevent hydrocephalus.

- Fractures associated with AVN are scaphoid, femoral neck, and talus fractures.
- Fractures associated with non-union are clavicular and fractures of the 5th metatarsal bone. (the biggest risk factor for non-union is smoking)
- Fractures associated with compartment syndrome are fractures of the tibia and supracondylar humerus.

- With epiphyseal fractures, only Type 1 and 2 fractures (the only ones that don't cross the epiphyseal plate) can be treated with a closed reduction.
- All the other ones (Types 3-5 fractures) require ORIF, because they cross the epiphyseal plate and can affect the growth plate.

- In the hands, the Radial nerve only provides sensation to the dorsal side of the first 3 ½ fingers.
- Sensation to the rest of the hand, both palmar and dorsum, is by the Ulnar nerve.

- Clavicular fractures can often be treated with just a sling, unless there is nerve or vessel injury, or unless the acromioclavicular joint is involved.

- Anterior shoulder dislocations have a risk of axillary nerve injury.
- Posterior shoulder dislocations have a risk of axillary artery injury.
- Both are treated with a closed reduction.

- Acromioclavicular separation has a risk of brachial plexus injury. Treatment is with a sling.

- Midshaft humerus fractures can be treated with a sling.
- Supracondylar humerus fractures should be treated with internal fixation in adults (closed reduction in kids).

- A "**Monteggia fracture**" is fracture of the proximal ulna with radial head dislocation. Treatment is an ORIF.

- A "**Colles fracture**" is a fracture of the distal radius, due to falling on outstretched hands. Treatment is closed reduction.

- Combined radius-ulna fractures in adults are best treated with an ORIF.

- **Scaphoid fractures** often have a negative X-Ray on initial presentation. Diagnosis is therefore clinical (tenderness in the anatomical snuffbox). Treatment is casting to the elbows.
- Scaphoid fractures carry a risk of AVN.

- "**Volkmann's syndrome**" is muscle contracture of the flexor compartment of the forearm, as a result of irreversible muscle necrosis.

- "**Dupuytren's contracture**" is contractions in the palm due to proliferation of the palmar fascia. It's associated with DM and alcohol.

- The rotator cuff muscles are: Supraspinatus, Infraspinatus, Teres minor, and Subscapularis.

- With any knee dislocation, need an angiogram to rule out popliteal artery injury.

- **Compartment syndrome** presents with the characteristic 6 P's: pain, paresthesia, pallor, paralysis, pulselessness, and poikilothermia.
- Pain in compartment syndrome is typically out of proportion to the injury, and is aggravated by passive stretching of the muscles within the affected compartment.
- The presence of a pulse does not rule out compartment syndrome, since pulselessness only rarely occurs (the pressure required to cause compartment syndrome is usually well below arterial pressures)

- The superficial peroneal nerve (in the lateral compartment) is involved in foot eversion, and provides sensation to the dorsum of the foot.
- The deep peroneal nerve (in the anterior compartment) is involved in foot dorsiflexion.

- **Osteomyelitis** is **MCly** caused by Staphylococcus. Diagnosis is with an MRI and treatment is with antibiotics (and possibly washout/debridement).

- "**Osgood-Schlatter disease**" is inflammation of the growth plate at the tibial tuberosity. It's **MC** in teens, and treatment is to limit physical activity. A knee immobilizer may be used for severe pain or to increase compliance.

- "**Legg-Calve-Perthes syndrome**" is AVN of the femoral head seen in infants, and it presents with a painful limp. It's bilateral 10% of the time and treatment is conservative.

- In "**Slipped capital femoral epiphysis**", there is instability of the proximal femoral growth plate, causing the femoral head to be displaced posteriorly and inferiorly in relation to the femoral neck.
- It carries an increased risk of AVN. Treatment is surgical internal fixation.

- Bone cancer is **MCly** metastatic in origin (**MCly** from the breast, followed by the prostate).
- Multiple myeloma is the **MC primary malignant** tumor of bone.
- Osteogenic sarcoma is the **MC primary sarcoma** of bone (classic "**Codman's triangle**" on X-Ray).

- "**Torus fracture**" is an impaction type of fracture, causing outward buckling/widening of the more proximal cortex due to the impaction.

- "**Greenstick fracture**" occurs in kids due to excessive bending of bone, as a result of blows to the shin or forearm (not to be mistaken with spiral/twisting fractures seen in abuse).

PEDIATRICS

- **Midgut** is the duodenum at level of the ampulla of Vater all the way to the distal 1/3 of the transverse colon.
- **Foregut** is proximal to the ampulla of Vater, and Hindgut is distal to the distal 1/3 of the transverse colon.

- Normal umbilical cord contains 1 vein (carrying blood in) and 2 arteries (carrying blood out).

- By definition, a low birth weight infant is any infant less than 2.5 kg at birth.

- A baby's immunity at birth comes from IgA's from the mother's breast milk, as well as IgM which the baby's body produces.

- The **MCC** of childhood death in the U.S. is trauma.

- The trauma bolus in Pediatric patients is 0.9% NS at 20 cc/kg twice, followed by blood at 10 cc/kg.

- In kids, tachycardia is the best indicator of shock.

- In neonates, normal heart rate is >150 bpm. In infants less than 1 year old, normal heart rate is >120 bpm. In a child over 1 year old, normal heart rate is >100 bpm.

- Infants less than 6 months old have about ¼ of the GFR that adults do.

- C. Diff is part of the normal flora in over half of asymptomatic neonates, and almost half of infants.

- The caloric requirement for infants less than 1 year old is ~100 kCal/day.
- Between 1 and 12 years old, it decreases to ~80 kCal/day.

- **Pulmonary sequestration** is lung tissue that has no communication with the tracheal tree. It can be connected to the pulmonary vasculature or to the systemic vasculature, and can be intralobular or extralobular.
- These present with respiratory compromise, and treatment is with a lobectomy.

- **Congenital lobar overinflation** results from cartilage failing to develop normally, causing air to get trapped in a pulmonary lobe. This can put pressure on remaining lung lobes. Treatment is with a lobectomy.

- **Congenital cystic adenoid malformation** (CCAM) of the lungs presents with absent bronchial cartilage and bronchial glands, and poorly developed alveoli. The symptoms are due to mass effect, and treatment is with a lobectomy.

- **Bronchogenic cyst** is the **MC** cystic lesion of the mediastinum.   It results in extrapulmonary cysts developing from bronchial tissue and/or bronchial cartilage. Symptoms are due to mass effect and treatment is resection of the cysts.

- **MCC** of a mediastinal mass **in kids** is a neurogenic tumor.
- **MCC** of an anterior mediastinal mass is Lymphoma.

- All **Choledochal cysts** require resection, due to the risk of cholangioCa, pancreatitis, and cholangitis.
- Type I is the **MC** type of Choledochal cyst and only involves the extrahepatic bile ducts.
- Type II is only a diverticulum, and the bile duct may therefore be preserved during resection.

- Type III involves the sphincter of Oddi. Treatment therefore requires a hepaticojejunostomy.
- Type IV and V involve intrahepatic bile ducts. Treatment may therefore require liver resections (type V is also known as "**Caroli's disease**").

- Asymptomatic lymphadenopathy is lymphoma until proven otherwise. Consider doing an excisional biopsy.

- **Cystic Hygromas** are lymph-filled sacs **MCly** in the posterior triangle of the neck, caused by poor lymphatic drainage.
- Complications include infection, webbed neck, lymphangioma (swollen lymph vessels), and (rarely) progression to hydrops and eventually fetal death.
- Initial treatment involves percutenaous drainage of the Cystic Hygroma to prevent facial deformities and airway obstruction. Definitive treatment requires surgical resection.

- **Diaphragmatic hernias** have a mortality rate of ~50%.
- Most are on the left, posterior side (**Bochdalek's**), and most have associated anomalies (usually cardiac or neural tube defects).
- (**Morgagni's** is located anteriorly and is rare)
- Treatment is with a surgical repair, but initial treatment involves medically stabilizing the patient with high-frequency ventilation, possibly ECMO, and prostacyclin (pulmonary vasodilation).

- **Branchial cleft cysts** can become infected or result in fistulas. Treatment can be conservative or resection.
- 1st branchial cleft cysts are at the angle of the mandible and may connect with the external auditory canal.
- 2nd branchial cleft cyst (**MC**) is between the SCM and the pharynx.
- 3rd branchial cleft cyst is in the lateral neck.

- **Thyroglossal duct cyst** results from the descent of the thyroid gland through the foramen cecum. Tissue in the thyroglossal duct cyst may be the only thyroid tissue a patient has.
- The **MC** location for a thyroglossal duct cyst is between the thyroid and the hyoid.
- Treatment is resection, sometimes requiring removal of part of the hyoid bone, and also the tract of the descent, due to the risk of infection and cancer.

- **Hemangiomas** have an initial rapid growth in the first 6-12 months of life, but then begin to go away. Treatment is observation, since most resolve by the age of 8.
- If it persists beyond childhood, or affects the ear canal or the eyelids, can try steroids. Laser therapy can be used if steroids are not successful.

Neuroblastoma:

- These are the **MC** solid abdominal cancers in kids, and the second **MC** solid cancers overall (the overall **MC** solid cancers in kids are brain cancers).

- Since these are of neuroendocrine origin (specifically of neural crest origin), they can arise from anywhere along the sympathetic chain, though they commonly originate in the adrenal glands.

- They are usually asymptomatic, but symptoms may include diarrhea, raccoon eyes (head metastases), HTN (from catecholamine release), and unsteady gait (bone metastases).

- In most cases, there are elevated catecholamine metabolites in the urine.

- Incidence is **MCly** at 1-2 years of age, and prognosis is typically poor, unless it is a low-stage, localized tumor that is caught early and resected.

- Neuron-specific enolase (NSE) is elevated in Neuroblastomas (since these tumors are of neuroendocrine origin). Levels are especially high if there are metastases.

- High Ferritin, high LDH, high NSE, diploid tumors, and N-Myc are all poor prognostic markers.

- Stage 1 is localized. Stage 2 is non-localized but does not cross midline. Stage 3 crosses the midline.

Wilms tumor:

- Typically diagnosed at ~3 years of age, and presents with hematuria and HTN.

- Histologically, Wilms tumor comprises of blast cells, mesenchymal cells, and epithelium cells.

- Undifferentiated tumors carry a poorer prognosis.

- Metastases are typically to the lungs and bones.

- Wilms tumor has some association with "**Beckwith-Wiedemann syndrome**".
- Beckwith-Wiedemann syndrome is characterized by hemihypertrophy, cryptorchidism, **Drash syndrome** (loss of playfulness, loss of appetite, loss of sleep), and aniridia.

- Treatment is nephrectomy and chemo/radiation depending on the Stage of the tumor.
- Tumor rupture during a nephrectomy worsens the prognosis due to possible spread.

- Stage 1 is limited to the kidneys. Stage 2 is beyond the kidneys, but contained. Stage 3 is lymph node involvement.

- All Stage 1 tumors <500g should get Actinomycin & Vincristine
- All Stage 1 tumors >500g, or all Stage 2 and higher, should also get Doxorubicin.
- All Stage 3 tumors also get radiation therapy.

Hepatoblastoma:

- Hepatoblastomas are the **MC** primary liver cancer in kids.

- It also has an association with Beckwith-Wiedemann syndrome.

- AFP is usually elevated.

- Prognosis is more favorable than with Hepatocellular Ca.

- Can present with precocious puberty as a result of the β-hCG released.

- Treatment is surgical resection, with or without pre-op chemo to reduce the size of the tumor.

- Prognosis is based on whether or not it's resectable.

In the Pediatric patients:

- **MC** cancer is leukemia (ALL).
- **MC** solid tumor in kids is brain tumor
- **MC** extracranial solid tumors is neuroblastoma
- **MC** liver tumor is Hepatoblastoma

- **MC** lung tumor is Carcinoid
- **MCC** of duodenal obstruction in <1 week is duodenal atresia
- **MCC** of duodenal obstruction >1 week is malrotation
- **MCC** of colonic obstruction is Hirschsprung's disease
- **MCC** of painful lower GI bleed is anorectal lesions/fissures
- **MCC** of painless lower GI bleed is Meckel's diverticulum

- **Meckel's diverticulum** arises from a persistent vitelline duct.
- The rule of 2's: 2 feet from ileocecal valve, 2% of population, and 2 types of tissue (pancreatic tissue is **MC**, gastric tissue is most likely to be symptomatic).
- Treatment is resection for symptomatic diverticula (diverticulitis or bleeding). If the diverticulitis involves the base of the Meckel's diverticulum, a segmental resection is required.

- **Pyloric stenosis** presents with projectile non-bilious vomiting. As a result of continued emesis, can get hypochloremic hypokalemic metabolic alkalosis, and sometimes paradoxical aciduria.
- Diagnosis is if the pyloric muscle is >4mm thick or >14mm long.
- Initial treatment is hydration and correction of the electrolyte abnormalities. A pyloromyotomy is eventually required.

- **Intussusception** presents with RUQ pain, vomiting and distention, as well as the "currant jelly stools" (due to vascular congestion) usually in 3 months to 3 years of age.
- Causes of intussusception in kids include enlarged Peyer's patches, lymphoma, and Meckel's diverticulum.
- Treatment is reduction with an air-contrast enema up to 120mmHg or barium enema up to a 1 meter high. Any more pressure and might risk perforating the bowel.
- If medical decompression fails, or if there is peritonitis or free air, then surgical reduction is required. This is done by applying pressure to the distal portion of the intussusception (not by pulling the proximal portion). Segmenetal resection of the affected area may be required if the cause is neoplastic (ex. Lymphoma).
- About 15% of intussusceptions will recur after reduction.
- (In an adult with intussusception, always consider a mass lesion (ex. Colon Ca), or possibly adult-onset Meckel's diverticulum)

- **Intestinal atresias** form due to intrauterine mesenteric vascular accidents.
- Similar to Hirschsprung's disease, intestinal atresia can also present with non-passage of Meconium.
- Of the intestinal atresias, duodenal atresia is associated with Down's Syndrome, polyhydramnios, and is also associated with cardiac, renal and other GI problems. It is usually distal to the ampulla of Vater and therefore causes bilious vomiting.
- Treatment of intestinal atresias is segmental resection.

Transesophageal fistulas (TEF):
- Type A: two blind pouches of the esophagus, with no connection to the trachea. Typa A is the **2ⁿᵈ MC** type of TEF.
- Type B: the proximal esophageal stump is connected to the trachea. Feeding therefore results in aspiration.
- Type C: the proximal esophageal stump is a blind end, no food therefore stays down. The distal esophageal stump is connected to the trachea. Type C is the **MC** type of TEF.
- Type D: both the prximal and distal esophageal stumps are connected to the trachea.
- Type E: the only type where the esophagus is continuous. It's basically a normal esophagus and normal trachea, connected by a fistula (also known as the "H" type). Type E is the **MC** TEF to present in adulthood.
- TEF's are a part of the "**VACTERL**" group of anomalies: **V**ertebral, **A**norectal, **C**ardiac, **TE** fistula, **R**enal, **L**imb.
- Treatment is an extrapleural thoracotomy with primary repair. The azygos vein may need to be ligated.

- If the infant is <2.5 kg or sick, delay the surgical repair of the TEF, and insert a G-tube for enteral nutrition.

- In normal fetal development, the GI undergoes a 270-degree counterclockwise (CCW) rotation.
- In **Malrotation**, this rotation does not occur as a result of "**Ladd's bands**", which originate in the right retroperitoneum.
- Any child with bilious vomiting needs an UGI to rule out malrotation. A pathognomic sign for malrotation on an UGI is contrast not crossing the midline.
- Treatment is resection of Ladd's bands, CCW rotation, cecopexy (anchoring the cecum to the abdominal wall), anchoring the duodenum to the RUQ, and removing the appendix.

- **Necrotizing enterocolitis** (NEC) is associated with prematurity and will often present with bloody stools. Need to obtain lateral decubitus films to look for free air.
- Treatment is medical, but if there is free air, peritonitis, or clinical deterioration, need to resect the portion(s) of dead bowel.

- **Imperforate anus** is more common in males, and is part of the "**VACTERL**" group of anomalies.
- A high-rising rectal pouch above the levator ani muscle requires a colostomy.

- **Gastroschisis** is due to an intrauterine rupture of the umbilical vein. It is not a midline defect, but rather occurs to the right of the midline.
- Treatment is to place a wet-gauze over the bowel and to medically stabilize the neonate. Once stabilized, an attempt can be made to place the bowel back in the abdomen, otherwise a silo can be used to cover the bowel and reduce it back into the abdomen over a prolonged period of time.

- **Omphalocele** is an embryonal developmental failure, causing a midline defect.
- Unlike Gastroschisis, the bowel in Omphalocele is covered by a sac. It can however present with a ruptured sac, so the lack of a sac does not rule out Omphalocele.
- It is associated with other congenital anomalies known as the "**Cantrell pentalogy**": Cardiac (VSD, cardiac ectopia), sternum (absence of lower sternum), pericardium (absence of a parietal pericardium), diaphragm (absent septum transversum causing a diaphragmatic hernia), and omphalocele.
- Treatment is the same as with gastroschisis: place a wet gauze over the bowel and medically stabilize the neonate. Once stabilized, can attempt to place the bowel back in the abdomen, otherwise insert the bowel in a silo.

- **Hirschsprung's** is the **MCC** of colonic obstruction in infants, and is more common in males. The diagnosis can be made with a contrast enema, but the gold standard is rectal biopsies to assess for the absence of ganglionic cells in the myenteric plexus.
- Treatment is resection of the affected colon, with either a primary anastomosis, or a two-stage repair with a stoma followed by a takedown at a future time.
- (C. Diff diarrhea may be the prominent symptom in a neonate with Hirschsprung's)

- **Umbilical hernias** in infants require surgery if the linea alba has not closed by age 5 or if it is an incarcerated hernia.

- **Inguinal hernias** in kids are due to a persistent processus vaginalis. They are more common in males and on the right side.
- Treatment is the same as with any other hernia; elective repair unless incarcerated.
- Because they are more common in males, girls with an inguinal hernia require bilateral groin exploration, and because they are more common on the right side, a left sided hernia repair requires exploration of the right side.

- **Biliary atresia** is the **MCC** of neonatal jaundice requiring surgery. Jaundice at over 2 weeks of age should raise suspicion for biliary atresia.
- Ultrasound and cholangiography can often reveal the biliary atresia, but a liver biopsy is sometimes required to assess for periportal fibrosis, bile plugging, and possibly cirrhosis.
- Complications associated with biliary atresia include cholangitis, cirrhosis, and hepatic failure. Treatment is therefore required ideally before 3 months of age to avoid irreversible liver damage. Treatment is the "**Kasai procedure**" (hepaticoportojejunostomy).
- About 1/3 of infants with biliary atresia die of the disease.

- **Osteosarcoma** is common, and commonly metastasizes to the lungs. Treatment involves resection of the primary tumor as well as resection of the lung metastases (if any).

- **Teratomas** have high AFP and β-hCG. In neonates we typically get sacrococcygeal teratomas, whereas in the elderly patients it's usually ovarian teratomas. Treatment is resection (ex. Coccygectomy).
- With the Sacrococcygeal teratomas seen in neonates, most are **benign** but have a malignant potential.
- 2 months of age is the key here, since most teratomas in infants older than 2 months old are malignant.

- With **undescended testicles**, wait until 2 years old to treat, since they may descend during that period.
- If it's undescended bilaterally, get chromosomal studies.
- The cancer risk (seminoma) remains high even if the testes are surgically brought down.
- If during surgery the testies can't be brought down, close and try again in 6 months.
- With undescended testies, and absent palpable testies in the inguinal area, need an MRI to see if the infant even has testies.

- "**Prune belly syndrome**" is a rare syndrome with abdominal wall hypoplasia, a dilated urinary system, and bilateral cryptorchidism.

- **Hydroceles** usually disappear by the first year of life. If it's still present after 1 year, treatment is hydrocelectomy, as well as ligation of the processus vaginalis.

- **Choanal atresia** (blocked nasal passage) is due to a bony or soft tissue formation during fetal development. Treatment is surgical perforation of the atresia.

- **Laryngomalacia** is the **MCC** of airway obstruction in infants. It presents with intermittent respiratory distress and stridor that worsens with a supine position.
- It's caused by an immature epiglottis cartilage resulting in occasional collapse of the epiglottis airway. Most will outgrow this by their teen years.

- **Laryngeal Papillomatosis** is the **MC** tumor of the larynx in children. It can be treated endoscopically with resection/laser but often recurs. It is thought to be due to HPV form the mother via the birth canal.

GI - GI HORMONES

- **Gastrin** is produced by G-cells in the antrum of the stomach, and acts on Parietal cells (HCl and IF release) and Chief cells (pepsinogen secretion)
- Its secretion is stimulated by CN10 (vagal, via gastric distention), alkali gastric content, Calcium and Alcohol.
- It's inhibited by acidic gastric content, somatostatin, secretin, CCK, VIP, and GIP.

- **Somatostatin** is produced by the D-cells of the antrum.
- Its secretion is stimulated by acid in the duodenum.

- **GIP** is produced by the K-cells of the duodenum, and acts on the Parietal cells of the stomach (decreases acid production), as well as the β-cells of the pancreas (increased insulin release).
- Its secretion is stimulated by nutrients (glucose, a.a., F.A.).

- **CCK** is produced by the I-cells of the duodenum, and causes gallbladder contractions (via PLC → IP3/ DAG → Ca+ release in the cell), relaxation of the sphincter of Oddi, increased pancreatic enzyme secretion, as well as insulin release.
- Its secretion is stimulated by a.a.'s and F.A.'s.

- **Secretin** is produced by the S-cells of the duodenum, and causes pancreatic bicarb release, increased bile flow, and inhibits gastrin release (decreases acid).
- Its secretion is stimulated by fat, bile, and acidic chyme.
- Its release is inhibited by gastrin.

- **Vasoactive Intestinal Peptide** (VIP) is produced by the pancreas, and causes increased intestinal secretions as well as increased GI motility.
- Its secretion is stimulated by fat and ACh.

- **Insulin** is released by the β-cells of the pancreas.
- Its secretion is not only stimulated by glucose, but also by CCK.

- **Glucagon** is produced by α-cells of the pancreas, and causes glycogenolysis, gluconeogenesis, lipolysis, ketogenesis, as well as decreased GI motility (to preserve energy).
- Its secretion is stimulated by hypoglycemia and ACh.

- **Pancreatic polypeptide** is produced by islet cells of the pancreas, and causes decreased pancreatic and gallbladder secretions.
- Its secretion is stimulated by food/gastric distention (vagal).

- **Motilin** is produced by cells of the GI tract, and causes increased motility.
- Its secretion is stimulated by acidic chyme and food/gastric distention.

- **Bombesin (Gastrin-releasing peptide)** causes increased motility, enzyme secretions, and gastrin secretion.

- **Peptide YY** is released from the terminal ileum following a fatty meal, and has the opposite effect of bombesin; decreases gallbladder/pancreatic secretion, decreases gastrin secretion.

GI - ESOPHAGUS

- The esophagus has no serosa.
- The top third is supplied by branches off the inferior thyroid artery (off the thyrocervical trunk).
- The lower/abdominal esophagus is supplied by the left gastric and inferior phrenic arteries.

- Lymphatics to the upper third drain cephalad, whereas the lower third drains caudad.

- The upper esophagus has striated muscle, whereas the lower esophagus has smooth muscle.

- The Phrenoesophageal membrane is an extension of the transversalis fascia. It comes off the diaphragm and covers the lower esophagus.

- The **right vagus nerve** travels on the posterior portion of the stomach, and becomes the celiac plexus. It has a "**criminal nerve of Grassi**", which can cause persistently high gastric acid levels post-operatively if it's undivided after a vagotomy.
- The **left vagus nerve** travels anterior to the stomach, and eventually ends in the liver/biliary tree.

- The upper esophageal sphincter (UES) is made up of the cricopharyngeus muscles, and is innervated by the recurrent laryngeal nerve.
- This is contracted at rest to prevent from swallowing air.
- The cricopharyngeus muscles are the **MC** site of esophageal perforation (usually as a result of an EGD).
- A brainstem stroke can prevent the UES from relaxing, and hence can cause food to go down the trachea instead.

- The lower esophageal sphincter (LES) is contracted at resting, and relaxes soon after initiation of swallow.
- It relaxes thanks to the stimulation of inhibitory neurons.

- Primary peristalsis occurs once a food bolus enters the esophagus
- Secondary peristalsis occurs with incomplete emptying of the esophagus, and continues indefinitely until the food bolus enters the stomach.
- Tertiary peristalsis is non-propagating and non-peristalsing (dysfunctional).

- The reflex arc of a hiccough is vagus n. $\rightarrow$ phrenic n. $\rightarrow$ sympathetic chain T6-T12.

- For heartburn, do an endoscopy, because can assess for esophagitis, etc.
- For dysphagia/odynophagia, do a barium swallow, because it's better at picking up masses.

- Trouble transferring food from the mouth to the esophagus is **MCly** a neuromuscular problem (ex. M-G, Parkinson's, Polymyositis, muscular dystrophy, Zenker's, stroke, etc). These are usually worse for liquids.

- Esophageal dysphagia at the cervical level, think **Plummer-Vinson syndrome**, which are webs due to Iron-deficiency anemia.
- Treat these webs with dilation and Iron, and screen for oral cancers.

- **Achalasia** is due to neuronal degeneration in the LES.
- It's not only characterized by failure of the LES to relax, but is also a lack of peristalsis.
- Treatment is calcium-channel blockers, β-blockers, nitrates, or LES dilation.
- If medical therapy and LES dilation fail, can do **Heller myotomy**: a left thoracotomy, transection of a circular layer of the lower esophageal muscle, and a partial Nissen fundoplication.

- Strong unorganized esophageal contraction with normal LES tone is pathognomic for **diffuse esophageal spasms**.
- Treatment is similar to the treatment of Achalasia: calcium-channel blockers, nitrates, and also can try antispasmodics. If this fails, do a Heller myotomy, though this is not as effective in diffuse esophageal spasms as it is for Achalasia.

- **Scleredema** often requires an esophagectomy. It causes strictures, fibrous replacement of the smooth muscle, and loss of LES tone.

Esophageal diverticula:

- **Zenker's diverticula** are not true diverticula, and occur due to increased swallowing pressure.
- They occur posteriorly between the pharyngeal constrictor muscles and the cricopharyngeus muscle.
- Diagnosis is with a barium swallow, since EGD can risk perforating it.
- Treatment is a cricopharyngeal myotomy. Removal of the diverticula is not necessary.
- Need an esophagogram on post-operative day one, to make sure it's sealed.

- **Traction diverticula** are true diverticula, and occur laterally, usually in the mid-esophagus.
- They are caused by inflammation, granulomatous disease, or tumor.
- Treatment is excision with a primary closure.

- **Epiphrenic diverticula** are rare, and are associated with motility disorders.
- They **MCly** occur in the distal 10 cm of the esophagus, and are usually asymptomatic.
- Treatment is diverticulectomy and long esophageal myotomy.

Gastroesophageal reflux disease (GERD):

- If there are symptoms of dysphagia or odynophagia with GERD, need to rule out a tumor.

- If there is associated bloating, need to rule out delayed gastric emptying, with a swallow study with follow-through.

- In an otherwise uncomplicated case of GERD, can try proton-pump inhibitors (PPI) for a month.
- If this fails, do an endoscopy with biopsies, to assess for strictures, Barrett's, etc.

- Surgery (ex. Nissen fundoplication) is indicated if PPI therapy fails, or if an endoscopy shows something suspicious.

- **Barrett's esophagus** is when squamous epithelium gets replaced by columnar epithelium.
- It can cause strictures, ulcerative bleeding, and increases the risk of AdenoCa by 50×.
- The presence of Barrett's esophagus is therefore an indication to do multiple biopsies. If there is carcinoma, or even high-grade dysplasia, it's an indication to perform an esophagectomy.
- Undilatable strictures are also an indication for surgery.

- **Low-grade dysplasia** can be treated like GERD (PPI, Nissen, etc).
- This will prevent further Metaplasia and esophagitis, but will not prevent cancer risk or cause regression of the already-occurred metaplasia.
- These patients therefore need life-long EGD's.

Hiatal hernias:

- **Type 1** is a sliding hernia. The gastroesophageal junction therefore slides up above the diaphragm.
- It is the **MC** type of hiatal hernia.
- Most patients with GERD have a Type 1 hiatal hernia, but most patients with Type 1 hiatal hernias do not

have GERD.
- Patients with **Schatzki's rings** almost always have a Type 1 hernia. Treatment of Schatzki's rings is dilation.

- **Type 2** is a paraesophageal hernia, where only the fundus of the stomach slides up.
- The gastroesophageal junction is therefore in the normal position, under the diaphragm.
- All Type 2 hiatal hernias need surgical treatment due to the high risk of incarceration.

- **Type 3** hiatal hernias are a combination of Type 1 and Type 2 hernias.

- **Type 4** hiatal hernias are also a combination of Type 1 and Type 2 hernias, but also have herniation of another abdominal organ.

Esophageal tumors:

- **Esophageal tumors** are almost always **malignant**, with invasion of nodes by the time of diagnosis.
- They spread quickly via submucosal lymphatic channels.

- The **MC** esophageal cancer is **AdenoCa** (not SCC), as a result of the secretory columnar epithelia seen in Barrett's esophagus.
- Since most esophageal cancers are due to chronic inflammation/Barrett's esophagus, they therefore **MCly** affect the lower esophagus.

- If there's hoarseness (RLN involvement), Horner's syndrome, phrenic nerve involvement, malignant pleural effusion, airway invasion, vertebral invasion, or any outside nodes/metastases... the tumor is not resectable.
- CT scan is the best test to assess for resectability.

- Metastases usually go to the lungs or the liver.

- **Esophagectomy** is only curative in about 20% of cases.
- The blood supply to the lower/abdominal esophagus is the left gastric artery and the inferior phrenic arteries. During an esophagectomy, the left gastric artery therefore has to be divided.
- Post-operatively, the main blood supply to the stomach is therefore the right gastroepiploic artery.
- After an esophagectomy, the stomach ends up in the chest, and its pylorus ends up just below the diaphragm. A pyloromyotomy therefore needs to be done with this procedure.

- With a young patient or with benign disease, may consider instead a colonic interposition, in order to preserve gastric function.

- Can also try Cisplatin and 5-FU for node-positive tumors or pre-operatively to shrink the tumor.

- **Benign** tumors of the esophagus are rare, and constitute <1% of all esophageal tumors.
- Leiomyomas are the **MC benign** tumors of the esophagus.
- Diagnosis is with an endoscopy, but no biopsies, because taking biopsies can form scars in the esophagus.
- If however the leiomyoma is >5cm, it requires a resection via endoscopic excision or thoracotomy.

- Esophageal polyps are another type of rare **benign** esophageal tumor.

Miscellaneous:

- With caustic esophageal injuries, first step is to take a CXR and an AXR to look for free air.
- If there is no clear evidence of perforation, do an endoscopy to look for perforation and to assess for injuries
- Avoid placing an NG tube, inducing vomiting, or giving anything by mouth, until a perforation has completely been ruled out.

- The **MC** site of an esophageal perforation after an EGD is the weakest site (at the Cricopharyngeus muscle).
- Diagnosis is with a Gastrografin swallow study.
- If contrast in the perforation is contained, and there are no systemic effects, then can treat non-surgically (fluid resuscitation, NPO, antibiotics).
- If the perforation is not contained, and it has been <24 hours since the perforation has occurred and there is minimal contamination, can treat with a primary repair with drains +/- intercostal muscle flap around the perforation.
- Otherwise if it has been >24 hours since the perforation, if there is contamination, or if the patient is unstable, a cervical esophagostomy is required to divert the food/spit, and a chest tube is required since these patients have a high leak rate. Can then later do an esophagectomy and gastric pull-up.

- "**Boerhaave's syndrome**" is esophageal perforation due to forceful vomiting.
- The perforation is usually lateral, and at the level of T8.
- We get here "**Hamman's sign**": mediastinal crunching on auscultation that is synchronous with the heartbeat.
- Diagnosis is with a Gastrografin swallow study.
- Treatment is with a thoracotomy, a longitudinal myotomy to assess the full extent of the esophageal injury, a primary repair, and placement of chest tubes.

- Food transit time in the stomach is usually about 3-4 hours.
- Peristalsis mainly occurs in the distal stomach. So in an antrectomy, we therefore get slowed gastric emptying.

- Pain in the stomach is sensed through afferent sympathetic nerves T5-T10.

- Smooth muscle relaxation (ex. hypokalemia, hypo/hypercalcemia, hypomagnesemia, hypothyroidism, etc) can cause delayed gastric emptying.

- The mucosa of the stomach is lined with simple columnar epithelium.

- Mucus is secreted in the stomach by the Cardia glands.

- Glands in the fundus and body include:
- **Chief cells**, which secrete Pepsinogen.
- **Parietal cells**, which secrete HCl and intrinsic factor (IF).

- ACh (CN10) and Gastrin act via Phospholipase to activate PIP → DAG → IP3 → increased Calcium, and hence PKC activation which results in increased HCl.
- Histamine acts on Adenylate Cyclase to increase cAMP → PKA, which results in HCl production.
- So both PKC and PKA promote HCl production.

- Glands in the antrum and pylorus include:
- Mucus and bicarb secreting glands that protect the stomach.
- **G cells**, which release gastrin.
- **D cells**, which release somatostatin.

- **MCC** of rapid gastric emptying is a previous surgery.
- **Zollinger-Ellison syndrome** (ZES) is the **MCC** of rapid gastric emptying in patients without previous surgeries.

- Phytobezoars are fibers, often found in diabetics due to the poor gastric emptying.

- **"Dieulafoy's ulcers"** are ulcers due to submucosal vascular malformations.

- **Ménétrièr's disease** is hyperplasia of the gastric mucosa, causing increased rugal folds. This can cause cancer.

- Gastric volvulus is rare, and is usually due to a paraesophageal hernia. Treatment is a Nissen fundoplication.

- **Mallory-Weiss tears** occur after forceful vomiting, and typically self-resolve.
- These tears are usually in the lesser curvature of the stomach, near the GE junction.
- Treatment is with a PPI and an EGD.
- If it still bleeds, may need surgery.

Vagotomies:

- **Truncal vagotomy** is when we divide the vagal trunks at the level of the esophagus.

- **Selective vagotomy** is when we divide the nerves of Latarjet (posterior) only.
- **Highly selective vagotomy** is when we divide individual fibers, hence dividing only those supplying the fundus/body. Here we get normal emptying of solids since the nerve fibers that supply the antrum are still intact. (Whereas in truncal or selective we also get decreased emptying of solids)

- All vagotomies accelerate liquid emptying, and the **MC** complication after a vagotomy is **diarrhea**.
- This is because there is no longer any sensation of bowel distention, and so the body thinks it's fasting. It therefore triggers sustained MMC's, which only occur during fasting, forcing bile acids into the colon.

- The decrease in acid production as a result of vagotomies causes Gastrin cell hyperplasia.

Upper GI bleeding:

- First thing to do is put in an NG tube and/or do an EGD to see if the bleeding is from an ulcer (because can potentially treat a bleeding ulcer with an EGD).
- If the patient is unstable despite resuscitation, then go to the OR.
- If an endoscopy can't identify the source of the bleeding, do a tagged RBC scan.
- Remember to assess for liver failure during the work-up, because the upper GI bleeding could be from esophageal varices.

Duodenal ulcers:

- This is more common than gastric ulcers, and is usually in the anterior part of the 1st part of the duodenum (right where the acidic chyme comes in).

- The anterior ulcers (**MC**) are more likely to perforate, whereas the posterior ulcers are more likely to bleed (due to the gastroduodenal artery posterior to it).

- 100% of duodenal ulcers have **H. Pylori**.
- A biopsy for H. Pylori needs to be from the gastric antrum, because that's where H. Pylori affects.
- Surgery is indicated if there is: perforation, refractory bleeding despite EGD attempts at controlling the bleed, obstruction, non-healing, and inability to rule out a cancer as the cause of the duodenal ulcer.

- If patient gets a duodenal ulcer depsite being on a PPI and/or H. Pylori eradication, an acid-reducing surgical procedure is required (ex. vagotomy).

- Make sure to rule out a Gastrinoma (**Zollinger-Ellison syndrome**) as the cause of the duodenal ulcers.

- Surgical treatment of duodenal ulcers:
- For **bleeding** not amenable to EGD treatment, do a duodenostomy with gastroduodenal artery ligation.

- For **obstructed** duodenal ulcers, serial dilation is the initial treatment of choice.
- If dilation fails, the stomach's contents need to bypass the obstruction, and hence do a Billroth 2/ gastrojejunostomy.
- If however the ulcer/obstruction is proximal to the ampulla of Vater, need to do an antrectomy with ulcer resection as well as a Billroth 2.

- For a **perforated** duodenal ulcer, do a primary repair and cover with a piece of omentum ("**Graham patch**").

- For refractory duodenal ulcers despite PPI for >3 months, do a highly selective vagotomy. This doesn't get 'rid' of the ulcer, but rather allows it to heal.

- **Zollinger-Ellison syndrome** is a disorder where increased levels of Gastrin are produced, typically by a gastrinoma, thereby resulting in ulcer formation.
- A 'secretin test', which usually suppresses gastrin release, increases gastrin levels in Zollinger-Ellison syndrome.

Gastric ulcers:

- **Type 1 gastric ulcers** are the **MC** type of gastric ulcer.
- They occur at the lesser curvature of the stomach, along the body.
- Types 1 and 4 are due to decreased mucosal protection.
- Treatment is a gastrectomy (including the ulcer), with Billroth +/- vagotomy.

- **Type 2 gastric ulcers** are at the lesser curvature and the duodenum.
- They are similar to duodenal ulcers, as in they are caused by high acid production.
- Treatment is a gastrectomy with Billroth +/- vagotomy.

- **Type 3 gastric ulcers** are prepyloric ulcers.
- Similar to Type 2 and duodenal ulcers, they are caused by high acid production.
- Treatment is a gastrectomy with Billroth +/- vagotomy

- **Type 4 gastric ulcers** are at the lesser curvature high along the cardia of the stomach.
- Types 1 and 4 are due to decreased mucosal protection.
- Treatment here is not gastrectomy, but rather simple ulcer excision +/- vagotomy.

- **Type 5 gastric ulcers** occur anywhere along the gastric gody, and are associated with NSAIDs.

- The proximal ones (types 1 and 4) are due to decreased mucosal protection, and are more common.
- The distal ones (types 2 and 3) are due to increased acid production.
- Most are on the lesser curvature of the stomach.

- Hemorrhage from gastric ulcers has a higher mortality than in duodenal ulcers.
- 80% of gastric ulcers are associated with H. Pylori (compared to 100% of duodenal ulcers).
- Type A blood is associated with Type 1 ulcers.
- Type O blood is associated with Types 2-4 ulcers.
- Surgical indications for gastric ulcers are the same as with duodenal ulcers: perforation, bleed, obstruction, cancer, and non-healing/refractory bleeding.

Gastritis:

- Stress gastritis occurs days after a stressful event. Treatment is with a PPI.
- If there is bleeding, then do an EGD or angiography.

- **Type A chronic gastritis** is at the fundus, and is associated with pernicious anemia and autoimmune diseases.
- This is because the fundus is where we have the Parietal cells that secrete IF.

- **Type B chronic gastritis** is at the antrum and is associated with H. Pylori.

Gastric cancers:

- Most **gastric cancers** are at the antrum, and they are more common in men.
- It's the cause of half of all cancer-related deaths in Japan.
- Risk factors include: polyps, smoking, previous gastric surgeries, pernicious anemia, type A blood, and nitrosamines.

- Gastric polyps have a 10-20% risk of cancer, and therefore need endoscopic resection.
- Treatment is a sub-total gastrectomy with 5cm margins.

- **Linitis Plastica** is diffuse gastric cancer, where the entire stomach has been invaded.
- Unlike gastric cancer, it is more common in women, has lymphatic invasion, and histology does not show any glands.
- It also has a less favorable prognosis than intestinal gastric cancer.
- Treatment is a total gastrectomy. It has a poor response to chemotherapy.
- If there have already been metastases, then surgery is contraindicated unless it's palliative (to treat obstruction, bleeding, pain).

- **Gastric leiomyomas** (GIST) are the **MC benign** gastric tumors.
- They are usually asymptomatic but can cause obstruction/bleeding.
- Treatment is resection with 1cm margins, but can also consider chemotherapy if the tumor is >5cm. Chemotherapy is with **Gleevec**, a Tyr Kinase inhibitor.
- Most of these are **c-kit** positive

- **Gastric leiomyosarcomas** are diagnosed based on the number of mitoses per HPF (>5-10 is diagnostic).
- These have hematogenous spread and treatment is en block resection due to its malignancy risk.

- **Gastric lymphomas** are the most common non lymph node lymphomas, and are usually non-Hodgkin's.
- Treatment, as with lymph node lymphomas, is with chemotherapy and radiation, and possibly surgical resection for Stage 1 disease (confined to mucosa).

- **Mucosa-associated lymphoproliferative tissue** (MALT) is related to H. Pylori infections, and is considered a precursor to Gastric lymphomas.
- It typically regresses after treating the H. Pylori. If it doesn't regress after eradicating H. Pylori, need chemotherapy.
- MALT is not only in the GI tract, but can also occur in the lungs and in Waldeyer's ring.

Bariatric Surgery:
- Eligibility for bariatric surgery is BMI >40, or >35 with comorbidities.
- Bariatric surgery has a mortality rate of ~1%.
- HTN does not always resolve after bariatric surgery, whereas sleep apnea, pseudotumor cerebri, GERD, and venous statis ulcers commonly resolve.

- **Roux-en-Y bypass** has better weight-loss outcomes than gastric stapling.
- Risks include **Vitamin B12 deficiency** (due to the lack of an acidic environment for IF to work), **Iron-deficiency** (since the duodenum is bypassed), and **cholelithiasis/cholecystitis** (as a result of the rapid blood loss, so do a cholecystectomy intraoperative if stones are present).
- Need to do an UGI study on post-operative day #2 to assess the anastomoses.
- **MCC** of roux-en-Y bypass failure is high carb/sugar snacking.
- **MCC** of an anastomotic leak is ischemia.

- **Jejunoileal bypass** is no longer done, because it's associated with liver cirrhosis, kidney stones, and osteoporosis.
- Treat these by converting to a Roux-en-Y.

Post-gastrectomy complications:
- **Dumping syndrome** occurs from carbs rapidly entering the small bowel, resulting in a hyperosmotic diarrhea, as well as a sudden surge in insulin causing hypoglycemia.

- This can almost always be treated conservatively with dietary changes: small, low-fat, low-carb, solid/non-liquid meals.

- **Alkaline reflux gastritis** usually occurs post-Billroth due to the lack of a pylorus.
- It presents with post-prandial epigastric pain, as well as nausea/vomiting.
- This is diagnosed with evidence of bile reflux into the stomach.
- Treat with Metoclopramide (improve gastric motility), cholestyramine, and H_2-blockers.
- Surgical options include converting the Billroth to a Roux-en-Y with >60cm of afferent limb.

- **Roux stasis** is when the chyme doesn't move through the small bowel due to the loss of jejunal motility.
- Treat with Metoclopramide or Erythromycin to increase motility. If this fails, can try surgery to decrease the length of the Roux limb.

- **Chronic gastric atony** can occur after a vagotomy.
- Treat with Metoclopramide to improve gastric motility.
- If this fails and the stomach just does not function, can do a near-total gastrectomy.

- A **small gastric remnant** causes early satiety, and can be managed with small meals, or treated surgically with a jejunal pouch construction.

- **Blind-loop syndrome** is due to bacterial overgrowth and stasis in the afferent limb, and presents with pain, diarrhea, and malabsorption.
- Treat with antibiotics for the bacterial overgrowth, and consider surgery to shorten the limb.

- **Afferent-loop syndrome** is obstruction of the afferent limb, and presents with epigastric/RUQ pain, vomiting (pain relieved with vomiting), and steatorrhea.
- Risk factors for this include a long afferent limb
- It's usually caused by recurrent ulcers, or due to technical/surgical error causing obstruction at the gastro-duo/gastro-jejuno anastomoses.
- Treatment includes balloon dilation, surgery to shorten the limb, or surgery to redo the anastomoses.
- If it occurs acutely, it's usually a complete obstruction, and is therefore a surgical emergency.

- **Efferent-loop syndrome** is obstruction of the efferent limb, and is treated with balloon dilation.

- **Postvagotomy diarrhea** is the **MC** complication post-vagotomy.
- It occurs because there is no longer any sensation of bowel distention, and so the body thinks it's fasting. It therefore triggers sustained MMC's, which only occur during fasting, forcing bile acids into the colon.
- Can treat with Cholestyramine to help absorb the bile acids and/or Octreotide to decrease the MMC's.

GI - LIVER

- The **MC** hepatic artery variant is a Right hepatic artery coming off the SMA.
- The **MC** variant of the Left hepatic artery is coming off the Left gastric artery.
- The **MC** variant of the Common hepatic is coming off the SMA.

- The **falciform ligament** separates the left lobe into medial and lateral segments (it does not separate the left and right lobe of the liver).

- **Ligament Teres** is the obliterated umbilical vein. It extends in the undersurface of the liver from the falciform ligament.

- The left and right liver lobes are separated by a line drawn from the middle of the gallbladder fossa to the IVC (so-called the "portal fissure" or "Cantalies line").

- Segment 1 is cephalad.
- Segment 2 and 3 are left most, left of the falciform ligament.
- Segment 4 is the medial portion of the left lobe, to the right of the falciform ligament.
- Segments 5 and 6 are inferior, to the right of the falciform ligament.
- Segments 7 and 8 are superior, to the right of the falciform ligament.

- The portal triad enters segment 4 of the liver.
- The gallbladder lies under segments 4 and 5.

- "**Glisson's capsule**" is the peritoneum that covers the liver.
- There is an area on the posterior-superior surface of the liver that is not covered by Glisson's capsule (called the bare area).

- **Triangular ligaments** are lateral and medial extensions of the coronary ligament on the posterior surface of the liver. These are made up of peritoneum.

- **Zone 1 hepatocytes** are closest to the portal vein, and therefore are the first to be exposed to incoming substrates. They therefore contain the highest amount of enzymes and nutrients, and are responsible for protein metabolism and gluconeogenesis.
- **Zone 3 hepatocytes** are the furthest from the portal vein, and therefore have a poorer oxygen supply. They are therefore involved in glycogenolysis and lipogenesis, which require low O_2.

- The **portal vein** is formed from the joining of the SMV and the splenic vein, and does not have valves.
- It can be accessed via the "**Kocher maneuver**", whereby the peritoneum lateral to the duodenum/pancreas is dissected, and the duodenum/pancreas is flipped to the left. From there the SMV can be seen, and followed cephalad to find the portal vein.

- Even though the portal vein supplies most of the blood flow to the liver, most tumors of the liver are supplied by the hepatic artery.

- The Left hepatic vein drains segments 2, 3, and the superior part of 4.
- The Middle hepatic vein drains inferior segment of 4 and segment 5.
- In most cases, the Middle hepatic vein joins the Left hepatic vein before draining into the IVC.
- The Caudate lobe drains segment 1, and drains directly into the IVC.

- Nutrient uptake occurs in sinusoidal membranes of the liver.
- ALP is located in canalicular membranes.

- Ketones and Urea are formed in the liver.

- Liver stores fat-soluble vitamins.
- The only water soluble vitamin stored in the liver is B12.

- Hepatocytes are the liver cells that are most sensitive to ischemia.

- Bilirubin is conjugated in the liver by the enzyme **Glucuronyl transferase**.
- Bilirubin can be broken down in the terminal ileum to give urobilinogen, which can be reabsorbed in the blood and released in the urine.

- **Bile** is mostly bile salts, with some cholesterol (bile acids), bilirubin, and Lecithin.
- Its final composition is determined by Na^+/K^+-transporters which reabsorb water in the gallbladder.
- Bile acids (made from cholesterol) can be conjugated to Taurine and Glycine to improve its water solubility.
- Lecithin is the main lipid in bile, and helps emulsify fats in the G.I.

- Jaundice usually occurs when bilirubin levels are >2.5.

- Hepatitis B is the only DNA hepatitis virus.
- Hepatitis E has a high risk of liver failure during pregnancy.
- Hepatitis C is the most common hepatitis virus requiring a liver transplant.

- With Hepatitis B vaccinations, a patient will only get anti-surface antibodies (no anti-core antibodies).
- The presence of anti-core and anti-surface antibodies, but no surface-antigens, means patient had an infection and then recovered and how has immunity.

- The **MCC** of SBP is E. Coli. If it's polymicrobial, need to worry about a bowel perforation.
- Treat SBP with a 3rd generation Cephalosporin.
- Risk factors for SBP other than liver failure/ascites include: nephrotic syndrome and SLE in children.

- Esophageal varices occur due to **coronary veins** in the lower esophagus that drain into the portal venous system.
- First-time bleeds have a ~30% mortality rate.
- The first-line treatment for esophageal varices is **sclerotherapy**. This can lead to strictures, which we can then treat by dilating.
- Medications that can be used include **vasopressin** (vasoconstriction; watch the BP in someone with a cardiac history) and **Octreotide** (decrease portal venous pressure).
- Can use a "**Sengstaken-Blakemore tube**" to control the bleeding. This is a enteral tube with a distal balloon that can be used to tamponade bleeding esophageal varices. It is hardly used anymore.
- **Propranolol** can be used to prevent rebleeding, but has no role in active bleeds.
- Refractory variceal bleeding will likely need a **transjugular intrahepatic portosystemic shunt** (TIPS), which is a shunt between the portal vein and the hepatic vein, thereby bypassing the liver.

- Normal **portal vein** pressure is <12 mmHg.
- Portal HTN can be divided into presinusoidal, sinusoidal, and post sinusoidal obstruction.
- Presinusoidal obstruction includes portal vein thrombosis, and schistosomiasis.
- Sinusoidal obstruction includes cirrhosis.
- Post sinusoidal obstruction includes Budd-Chiari syndrome (hepatic vein thrombosis), and CHF.

- **Transjugular intrahepatic portosystemic shunt** (TIPS) is the treatment of choice for refractory variceal bleeding and refractory ascites. It can however worsen encephalopathy, because it eliminates first-pass metabolism.
- A **splenorenal shunt** is another option, but it's rarely used anymore. It has less risk of encephalopathy than TIPS, but has a higher risk of ascites. It's therefore only considered for "**Child's A cirrhosis**", which is the least severe type of cirrhosis, and the only one without ascites.

- Portal HTN in kids is usually caused by presinusoidal/extrahepatic portal vein thrombosis.
- It's the **MCC** of massive hematemesis in kids.

- **Budd-Chiari syndrome** is hepatic vein thrombosis.
- Treatment is a portacaval shunt, where the connection has to be high enough in the IVC to be above the venous occlusion.

- **Splenic vein thrombosis** can lead to gastric varices, with normal portal venous pressures in the rest of the portal venous system.
- It can be caused by pancreatitis.
- Treatment is a splenectomy (it is one of the few indications for a splenectomy).

Liver failure:

- **Cirrhosis** is the **MCC** of liver failure.
- It is caused by hepatocyte destruction, leading to fibrosis/scarring.
- The best indicator of synthetic function in a cirrhotic patient is the **Prothrombin Time** (PT).
- Treatment for liver cirrhosis include: limiting protein intake (to decrease Urea) and tapping the ascites to rule out SBP.
- When limiting protein intake, branched chained a.a.'s are ok, because they are metabolized by skeletal muscle.
- Prophylatic antibiotic therapy is not required in liver cirrhosis.
- **Acute fulminant hepatic failure** has an 80% mortality rate, the outcome of which is determined by the course of the encephalopathy.
- **Hepatic encephalopathy** is treated with **lactulose**, which is a cathartic that gets rid of bacteria in the gut and acidifies the colon, thus preventing NH_3 uptake by converting it to NH_4.

- With **ascites**, when doing a paracentesis, replace the ascitic output with 1g of Albumin for every 100cc of ascites taken out.
- Treat ascites with Spironolactone (counteracts the hyper-aldosteronism seen in liver failure due to impaired hepatic metabolism of aldosterone), water restriction, a peritoneovenous shunt (LeVeen shunt), and consider prophylactic antibiotics.

- **Hepatorenal syndrome** is via the same mechanism as pre-renal azotemia, so treat by giving fluids and stopping diuretics.

- Post-partum liver failure +/- ascites is due to hepatic vein thrombosis.

Benign liver tumors:

- **Hepatic adenomas** are seen with OCP use, steroid use, and type 1 collagen diseases.
- Most are asymptomatic, but they can rupture/bleed, and can also become malignant.
- They are more common in the right lobe of the liver.
- Histologically, there are no Kupffer cells in adenomas, and hence no uptake on a "**sulfur colloid scan**" (i.e. they're said to be 'cold', or non-functional).
- For asymptomatic liver adenomas, treatment is to simply stop the steroids/OCP's. If it doesn't regress, it needs to be resected.

- If it's symptomatic, it needs to be resected.
- If they are multiple and therefore unresectable, they need to be embolized.

- **Focal nodular hyperplasia** has no malignancy risk, and is unlikely to rupture.
- It has Kupffer cells on histology, and so unlike hepatic adenoma, it will take up sulfur colloid on a scan.
- Treatment is conservative.

- **Hemangiomas** are the **MC benign** hepatic tumor.
- Most of these are asymptomatic, and rupture is rare.
- Avoid doing a biopsy because of the risk of hemorrhage.
- Treatment is conservative unless it's symptomatic, then a resection is required.
- A rare complication of hemangiomas in kids is consumptive coagulopathy ("**Kasabach-Merritt syndrome**").

- Solitary cysts need to be resected only if they are bleeding or are infected, and percutaneous drainage is not possible.
- Most liver cysts though can be left alone.

Malignant liver tumors:

- **Hepatocellular Ca** is the **MC** cancer worldwide.
- Risk factors include Hepatitis B and C, alcohol, hemochromatosis, primary sclerosing cholangitis, aflatoxins, hepatic adenomas, and pesticides.
- Primary biliary cirrhosis and Wilson's disease are not risk factors.
- Best prognosis is with clear cell, lymphocyte infiltrative, and fibrolamellar types
- AFP levels often correlate with tumor size.
- Even with a resection, 5-year survival is fairly low (30%) due to the high likelihood of recurrence, and also metastases.

- **Hepatic sarcoma** risk factors include PVC, arsenic, and thorotrast exposure. It is rapidly fatal.

- **Cholangiosarcoma** risk factors include clonorchiasis infection, U.C., choledochal cysts, hemochromatosis, and primary sclerosing cholangitis.
- Intrahepatic cholangiosarcomas have a worse prognosis than extrahepatic. Large tumor size is also associated with a worst prognosis.

- With Colon Ca metastases to the liver, can resect it, but will still have a low 5-year survival rate (~20%).
- Survival rate is worsened with >3 metastases, metastases >5cm, or CEA >200.
- Liver resection of metastatic colon Ca should only be considered if the primary tumor is controlled, there are no other metastases in the body, and if the liver metastases are resectable.
- If it's non-resectable, can debulk for pain control, or possibly embolize angiographically.

- Primary liver tumors are typially hypervascular, whereas metastatic liver tumors are hypovascular.

Liver abscesses:

- **Amebic abscesses** come from a primary infection in the colon, via the portal vein.
- Risk factors for this include travel to an exotic country, and alcohol abuse.
- Many patients with liver amebic abscesses have positive serology for Entamoeba Histolytica (which causes amebic colitis).
- Cultures of the abscess are usually negative, since the protozoa live in the periphery of the abscess.
- Treatment with **Metronidazole** is usually sufficient. Otherwise can try percutaneous aspiration, or surgery if the amebic abscess ruptures.

- **Echinococcus** forms so-called "hydatid cysts".
- Patients with Echinococcus test positive to the "**Casoni skin test**", and positive indirect hemagglutination.
- Sheep and dogs carry Echinococcus.
- Do not aspirate the hydatid cysts, because they can leak and cause an anaphylactic shock.
- CT scan of the hydatid cysts shows a calcified external layer.
- Treatment is surgical resection (including the cyst wall) and preoperative **Albendazole**.

- **Schistosomiasis** presents with eosinophilia and a rash.
- Patients might also get sigmoid colon complications, such as ulcers, obstruction, and cancer.
- Treatment is **Praziquantel**.

- **Pyogenic abscesses** account for most liver abscesses.
- The **MC** organism is E. Coli, usually due to a contiguous infection from the biliary tract.
- Diagnosis is via aspiration/culture, and treatment is with a CT-guided drainage and antibiotics.
- If the patient is unstable, surgery might be required.

GI - BILIARY SYSTEM

- The "**Triangle of Calot**" is bordered by the cystic duct laterally, the CBD medially, and the liver superiorly.
- Cystic veins drain into the portal venous system.
- The gallbladder's mucosa is columnar epithelium. It has no submucosa.

- CCK causes constant, steady tonic gallbladder contractions. That by itself is enough to secrete bile into the GI.
- The biliary ductal system itself does not have peristalsis.

- The gallbladder fills by simply having the sphincter of Oddi contracted.
- Morphine contracts this sphincter. Glucagon relaxes it.

- Normal CBD size is <8mm.
- Normal gallbladder wall thickness is <4mm.

- "**Rokitansky-Aschoff sinuses**" are invaginations of the epithelium of the wall of the gallbladder, caused by increased gallbladder pressure.
- They are associated with Adenomyomatosis (an intramural gallbladder diverticulum). This is not malignant, nor does it cause stones.

- "**Ducts of Luschka**" are small bile ducts that go from the liver directly to the gallbladder.

- Bile is produced in the liver by hepatocytes (main source of bile), and by bile canalicular cells.

- Bile in the gallbladder gets concentrated as a result of water reabsorption, thanks to Na^+/K^+-antiports.

- Conjugated bile acids can get reabsorbed in the terminal ileum.

- The color of bile comes from conjugated bilirubin.
- This conjugated bilirubin can be broken down in the gut to give Stercobilin (brown color of stool), and Urobilin (reabsorbed and gives yellow of urine).

- HMG-CoA is converted to Cholesterol by the rate-limiting enzyme **HMG-CoA Reductase**.
- Cholesterol is then converted to bile acids thanks to **7-α-Hydroxylase**.
- In overweight patients, stones are usually due to an overactive HMG-CoA Reductase
- In thin patients, stones are usually due to an underactive 7-α-Hydroxylase.

- **Hemobilia** is due to a fistula between the bile duct and the hepatic arterial system. It therefore presents with RUQ pain, and UGI bleed.
- It occurs **MCly** as a result of trauma, infections, stones, and tumors.
- First-line treatment is angiography with embolization. If this fails, surgery is required.

Gallstones:

- Gallstones occur in ~10% of the population, but they are usually asymptomatic.

- **Nonpigmented stones** are the **MC** type of gallstone in the U.S.
- They are due to decreased solubility of cholesterol as a result of: stasis, increased water reabsorption, decreased lecithin in bile acids, or increased mucin glycoproteins secretion by the gallbladder mucosa (too much mucin glycoproteins can promote stone formation).

- **Pigmented stones** are the **MC** type of gallstone worldwide, and are due to precipitation of calcium bilirubinate. They can be black or brown:
- **Black pigmented stones** are due to hemolytic disorders, cirrhosis, long-term TPN, or in patients with an ileal resection. The common factor here is increased bilirubin.
- **Brown pigmented stones** are due to infections (E. Coli **MC**, but also parasites), which de-conjugate the bilirubin via the enzyme β-glucuronidase, forming calcium bilirubinate.
- These form in the bile ducts, so treatment requires an ERCP/sphincteroplasty, and antibiotics/antiparasitics.
- In Oriental countries, parasites such as C. Sinensis, A. Lumbricoides, and T. Trichiura can cause recurrent brown pigmented primary CBD stones, and hence recurrent cholangitis. This causes what's known as "Oriental Cholangiohepatitis". Treatment for these recurrent cases is a hepaticojejunostomy.

- **Gallstone ileus** is bowel obstruction due to a gallstone that gets in the GI tract via a gallbladder-duodenal fistula.
- The obstruction by the gallstone is usually at the ileo-cecal valve.
- Treatment of gallstone ileus is to resect the stone via an enterotomy proximal to the obstruction, by doing a fistula resection, as well as a cholecystectomy.

Cholecystitis:

- Brown pigmented stones are not a risk factor for cholecystitis, because they can't obstruct the cystic duct since they are biliary duct stones.
- U/S is the best initial test to diagnose cholecystitis: look for gallbladder wall thickening and pericholecystic fluid.

- In ill patients who are not surgical candidates, a cholecystostomy tube can be placed temporarily instead of doing a cholecystectomy.

- An indication for a pre-operative ERCP is if there is a CBD stone present.

- **Air in the biliary system** with no history of ERCP, can be due to cholangitis, or can be due to an enteric fistula.
- Treatment of a biliary-enteric fistula is a cholecystectomy, and closure of the bowel where the fistula originates.

- **Air in the gallbladder** wall can be Clostridium Perfringens. Diabetics have a high risk of this.
- It can lead to gallbladder perforation, and so treat with an emergent cholecystectomy, or percutaneous drainage if the patient is not a surgical candidate.

- **Acalculous cholecystitis** occurs **MCly** after burns, prolonged TPN, trauma, major surgery, narcotics, or fasting.
- It is due to bile stasis and/or increased viscosity (dehydration).
- U/S shows the same thing as in cholecystitis, except no stones here.
- HIDA scan is positive here. So consider a HIDA if there is sonographic Murphy's sign/edema/wall thickening, but no stones identified.

Lap Chole complications:
- **Common bile duct injuries** occur much more commonly laparoscopically
- Intraoperative cholangiography allows early diagnosis of a bile duct injury.
- In ~10% of cases, the cystic duct is confused with a right posterior bile duct (from segments 6 and 7) that enters the CBD separately.
- If the CBD injury is less than half the circumference, it can be repaired primarily. Otherwise will need a hepaticojejunostomy.

- With persistent nausea/vomiting or jaundice following a lap chole, do an U/S.
- If the U/S shows a fluid collection, it may be caused by a **bile leak**. Treatment is percutaneous drainage.

- If the fluid is bilious, it's likely a cystic duct leak, so do an ERCP. If it turns out that it is in fact a cystic duct leak, can put a stent in the CBD to occlude the opening of the CBD into the cystic duct.
- If the U/S shows no fluid collection, but dilated intrahepatic ducts, and labs show hyperbilirubinemia, then there may be a **ligated CBD**. Treatment is a hepaticojejunostomy.
- Sepsis following a lab chole may be due to a ligated CBD.
- The CBD can also just be strictured. So in that case just do an ERCP with stent placement.

- With **shock** following a lap chole, stabilize the patient first.
- Within the first 24 hours, shock may be due to hemorrhaging as a result of a clip that fell off the cystic artery.
- After the first 24 hours, shock is most likely septic shock from a ligated CBD.

- Can also have **retained stones** in the CBD after a Lap Chole.
- Treatment is endoscopic sphincterotomy.
- Surgery is indicated if the retained stone is due to a distal CBD stricture, if there's a history of Billroth II procedure (hard to do an ERCP after a Billroth procedure), or if there's been a recent episode of pancreatitis (avoid ERCP with a recent history of pancreatitis).

- **Bile duct strictures** occur commonly after lap chole's, usually due to ischemia. It can also be caused by local inflammation (like with pancreatitis).
- Treatment is ERCP sphincterotomy +/- stent placement.
- If however it occurs within 7 days post-operatively, it's unlikely to be managed with an ERCP due to post-operative inflammation, so need to do a hepaticojejunostomy.
- If it occurs many years later, on top of treating it with ERCP/stenting, need to rule out cancer as the cause of the strictures, since it is then unlikely to be a complication of the lap chole.

Gallbladder adenoCa:

- Adenocarcinoma of the gallbladder is the **MC** cancer of the biliary system.
- The liver is the **MC** site of metastases (segments 4 and 5 specifically).
- **Porcelain gallbladder** (calcification of the gallbladder) is a risk factor for gallbladder adenoCa, so patients with porcelain gallbladder need a cholecystectomy.
- Stage 1 gallbladder adenoCa (confined to the mucosa) only requires a cholecystectomy.
- Stage 2 gallbladder adenoCa (spread into the submucosa) requires a wide resection around the liver bed, regional lymphadenectomy, and possibly resection of the CBD.
- There is a high risk of tumor implantation at the laparoscopy trocar sites. For this reason laparoscopy is contraindicated if it's known before-hand that there is gallbladder cancer.
- Because patients with gallbladder adenoCa are often asymptomatic, they often present at Stage 4 (metastases).

Bile duct Ca (CholangioCa):

- Risk factors for CholangioCa include ulcerative colitis (U.C.), Choledochal cysts, sclerosing cholangitis, typhoid, and Clonorchis Sinensis infection
- It has early invasion to local structures.
- Biliary stenosis in a patient with no history of surgery/pancreatitis is suggestive of bile duct Ca.
- "**Klatskin tumor**" is the **MC** type (and unfortunately the worst prognosis), and it's when cholangioCa occurs at the confluence of the right and left hepatic ducts.
- If the tumor is halfway down the CBD, can do a hepaticojejunostomy.
- If the tumor involves the lower third of the CBD, need a Whipple since it likely involves the ampulla of Vater.
- If it's unresectable, place a stent for palliation.

Choledochal cysts:

- Discussed in more detail in the *Pediatric Surgery* section.
- All choledochal cysts need to be resected, due to the risk of cholangioCa, pancreatitis, and cholangitis.

Primary sclerosing cholangitis:

- Occurs mostly in men.
- It is associated with U.C., cholangioCa, Riedel's thyroiditis, pancreatitis, and DM.
- Can lead to pressure build-up in the bile duct, and hence can eventually lead to liver failure and portal HTN.
- Diagnosis is with an ERCP, showing alternating areas of stricture and dilation (bead appearance).
- Often get **anti-neutrophilic cytoplasmic antibodies** (p-ANCA) and **anti-smooth muscle antibodies**.
- Cholangitis in primary sclerosing cholangitis is not infectious, but rather inflammatory.
- Even though it is associated with U.C., it does not get better after a colectomy.
- The only definitive treatment is a liver transplant, but a choledochojejunostomy may be effective for some patients.
- Can also try balloon dilation of the strictures.
- Cholestyramine and Ursodeoxycholic acid can decrease bile acids and hence improve symptoms.

Primary biliary cirrhosis:

- This occurs mostly in women.
- Often get **anti-mitochondrial antibodies**.
- This has no risk of malignancy (unlike primary sclerosing cholangitis)
- Symptoms are the same as with primary sclerosing cholangitis, and hence treatments are the same.
- Similar to primary sclerosing cholangitis, transplant is the only definitive long-term treatment.

Cholangitis:

- Cholangitis presents with **Charcot's triad**: RUQ pain, jaundice, and fever.
- **Reynold's pentad** is when we also get mental status change and shock (due to sepsis).
- Gallstones are the biggest risk factor for cholangitis.
- Other risk factors include: cancer, strictures (from previous surgeries), chronic pancreatitis, and choledochal cysts.
- The most serious complication is renal failure as a result of the sepsis.
- Treatment is fluid and antibiotics.
- If the cholangitis is due to a gallstone, treatment involves an emergent ERCP with stone extraction. If there is a stone but can't extract it with an ERCP, a percutaneous cholecystostomy tube is required.

Miscellaneous:

- **Granular cell myoblastoma** is a **benign** neuroectoderm tumor of the gallbladder, with symptoms of cholecystitis.
- Treatment is cholecystitis.

- **Cholesterolosis** is a change in the gallbladder wall due to excess cholesterol.
- It results in speckled cholesterol deposits on the gallbladder wall.

- **Gallbladder polyps** are worrisome if they are >1cm, or if the patient is >60 years old.
- Otherwise if they are <1cm, they are likely benign, and treatment is observation.

- **Delta bilirubin** is conjugated bilirubin that is covalently bound to albumin.
- Because it is protein-bound, it is not excreted by the kidneys, and therefore has a long $t_{1/2}$ (~18 days).
- It may be responsible for the persistent bilirubinemia seen in patients with cholestasis.

- "**Mirizzi syndrome**" is stenosis of the CBD by either gallstones, or scar/inflammation from chronic cholecystitis.

GI - PANCREAS

- The SMA and the SMV lie behind the pancreas.

- The head of the pancreas is supplied by the superior and inferior pancreaticoduodenal arteries (each one of these having anterior and posterior branches).
- The body and tail of the pancreas are supplied by the great/inferior/caudal pancreatic arteries as well as the left gastroepiploic arteries, all of which are off the splenic artery.

- Ductal cells of the pancreas have **Carbonic Anhydrase** (CA).
- Slow flow of pancreatic secretions allows for CA to work, hence reabsorbing HCO_3, which is why slow duct flow results in low bicarb/high Cl⁻ secretions.

- Acinar cells of the pancreas secrete digestive enzymes.

- **Amylase** is the only pancreatic enzyme that is secreted in an already-active form.
- It hydrolyzes the α-1-4 links between glucose chains.
- Salivary amylase is inactivated by gastric juices, and so pancreatic amylase takes over in the small bowel.

- **Glucagon** (α-cells), **insulin** (β-cells), **somatostatin** (delta-cells), **pancreatic polypeptide** (F-cells), and **VIP** (islet cells) are all made in the pancreas.

- In relation to their size, Islet cells receive the most blood supply compared to the other pancreatic cells.

- **Enterokinase** released by the duodenum activates Trypsinogen to Trypsin, which in turn activates all other pancreatic enzymes (including itself).

- **Secretin** (made in the duodenum) increases pancreatic bicarb secretion.
- CCK (made in the duodenum) increases pancreatic enzyme secretion.
- ACh does both.

- Embryologically, the ventral pancreatic bud (which has the **duct of Wirsung** – main duct) migrates over and behind the duodenum ('clockwise') to fuse with the dorsal bud (which has the **duct of Santorini** – accessory duct).
- This causes the 2 ducts to fuse. The dorsal duct is the "main" duct, but the ventral opening into the duodenum is the "main" opening.

- An **annular pancreas** occurs when the ventral bud fails to do a clockwise rotation.
- It is associated with Down's syndrome.
- Treatment is a duodeno-duodenostomy or duodenojejunostomy.
- The pancreas does not need to be resected in annular pancreas, since it is fully functional.

- **Pancreas divisum** is when the two pancreatic ducts fail to fuse, so that each duct drains into the duodenum separately.
- In pancreas divisum, even an accessory duct (Santorini) stenosis can cause pancreatitis.
- Diagnose this with an ERCP, which will show a long and large duct of Santorini (dorsal/main bud) in the minor papilla and only a short duct of Wirsung (ventral bud) in the major papilla.

Pancreatitis:

- Stones and alcohol are the **MC** causes of acute **pancreatitis** in the U.S.

- Pancreatitis can cause pleural effusions, as well as ileus due to the inflammation.

- **"Grey-Turner sign"** is flank ecchymosis. **"Cullen's sign"** is periumbilical ecchymosis. **"Fox's sign"** is inguinal ecchymosis.

- The pathogenesis of pancreatitis is mostly due to pre-activation of degradation enzymes, leading to autodigestion.
- Without a specific cause for pancreatitis, need to rule out malignancy.

- Acute pancreatitis has a mortality rate of 10%. Hemorrhagic pancreatitis has a mortality rate of 50%.

- If 8 **Ranson criteria** are met, there is a 100% mortality risk.
- Early Ranson criteria include: >55 yo, WBC >16, Glucose >200, AST >250, LDH >350.
- Late Ranson criteria include: low Hb, low Calcium, high BUN, and high Creatinine.

- Do an U/S to look for stones and/or CBD dilation, and an abdominal CT scan to assess for pancreatic necrosis.

- Amylase levels do not correlate with the severity of the pancreatitis, especially in chronic pancreatitis.
- Falsely elevated Amylase can occur in small bowel infarction, perforated duodenal ulcers, gangrenous cholecystitis, and hyperlipidemia.

- Treatment of pancreatitis is NPO, fluids, and antibiotics. If it's gallstone pancreatitis, do an ERCP +/- sphincterotomy.
- With necrotizing pancreatitis (due to phospholipase release), if it's sterile, no specific treatment is required. The only indication for surgery is an infected necrotizing pancreatitis, since CT-guided drainage of a pancreatic abscess is usually not effective.
- Obesity is the biggest risk factor for necrotizing pancreatitis.

- Mildly elevated amylase/lipase does not necessarily mean there's pancreatitis. It can simply be due to cholecystitis, sialoadenitis, SBO, or ischemic bowel.

- **Chronic pancreatitis** can cause irreversible parenchymal calcification and fibrosis.
- Alcohol is the **MC** cause, though the cause is often unknown.
- Islet cells are often preserved in chronic pancreatitis
- Characteristic here is an alternating dilated and stenosed pancreatic duct.
- Treatment is mostly supportive.
- Surgery is indicated for biliary obstruction, abscess, or pain affecting the quality of life, and consists of a **"Puestow procedure"**, also known as a pancreaticojejunostomy.
- Chronic pancreatitis is the **MCC** of splenic vein thrombosis, which can present as bleeding from gastric varices that form as collaterals. This is an indication to perform a splenectomy.
- Chronic pancreatitis can also cause CBD strictures.

- **Pancreatic pseudocysts MCly** occur in patients with chronic pancreatitis, and **MCly** occur at the head of the pancreas.
- Symptoms include pain, fever, weight loss, and bowel obstruction due to compression.
- Small cysts <5cm usually resolve spontaneously.
- For larger cysts, monitor for 3 months, to allow the pseudocyst to mature. Then only treat the pseudocyst if there are symptoms or if it is still growing, by first doing an ERCP/MRCP.
- If there is no pancreatic duct involvement, do a percutaneous drainage of the pseudocyst.
- If there is pancreatic duct involvement, need to do a cystogastrostomy (anastomose the pancreatic cyst to the stomach) to allow for drainage.
- If a pancreatic cyst is found incidentally, and the patient has had no history of pancreatitis, and the cyst is not purely serous, need to resect it.

- **Pancreatic fistulas** usually resolve spontaneously. Treat these by allowing the fistula to drain.
- Somatostatin sometimes works to decrease the pancreatic output.
- If this fails, for distal pancreatic fistulas can do a distal pancreatectomy. For proximal pancreatic fistulas, can do a Whipple's.

- **Pancreatic insufficiency** (like with chronic pancreatitis) will present with steatorrhea and/or malabsorption.
- Treat with a low-fat diet and pancreatic enzyme replacement.

Pancreatic AdenoCa:

- Pancreatic adenoCa is more common in males, and the **MC** symptom is weight loss.
- The biggest risk factor is smoking.
- Even with resection, the 5 year survival rate is ~20%.
- The serum marker in pancreatic cancer is **CA-199**.
- Pancreatic Ca has more lymphatic spread than hematologic spread.

- Most of these are at the head of the pancreas.
- Most of these are ductal AdenoCa. The tumors of the exocrine pancreas have a more favorable prognosis.

- Half of these are unresectable at the time of diagnosis, because they have already invaded neighboring structures, including lymph nodes, or have regional or distant metastases.
- When it is a resectable mass, we do not need a biopsy, since it will be resected anyway. Only do a biopsy in suspected pancreatic adenoCa metastases in other orgrans.
- During the resection, first check the space between the posterior pancreas and the anterior portion of the SMV/Portal vein, to check for local invasion. If there is invasion, the tumor is unresectable.

- Dilation of both the pancreatic duct and the CBD on a CT scan is characteristic of pancreatic adenoCa.
- A dilated pancreatic duct in itself is not indicative of pancreatic cancer, because it can result from chronic pancreatitis.
- ERCP can tell pancreatic cancer apart from chronic pancreatitis, because only cancer will have a duct with irregular narrowing, displacement, and destruction.

- Complication of **Whipple's** is **MCly** delayed gastric emptying. Can treat this with Metoclopramide.
- Management of bleeding post-Whipple's, is initially embolization via interventional radioloy, because bleeding is hard to control in a re-do operation since the tissue becomes very friable.

- Consider doing a celiac plexus block for painful unresectable disease.

Nonfunctional endocrine tumors:

- Nonfunctional endocrine tumors are not as common as functional endocrine tumors.
- Symptoms are similar to pancreatic adenoCa.
- Most of these are **malignant**, but have a slower course than pancreatic adenoCa.
- Diagnosis can be made with a CT/MRI.
- Similar to pancreatic adenoCa, treatment is resection unless there are metastases.
- Liver is the **MC** site of metastases.
- 5-year survival after resection is ~50% (compared to 20% for adenoCa).
- 5-FU and Streptozocin can be effective.

Functional endocrine tumors:

- Functional endocrine tumors represent the majority of the pancreatic endocrine tumors.

- They include: insulinomas, gastrinomas, glucagonomas, somatostatinomas, and VIPomas.
- Gastrinomas and somatostatinomas occur **MCly** in the pancreatic head.
- **Octreotide** is effective against insulinomas, gastrinomas, glucagonomas, and VIPomas.
- All functional endocrine tumors respond well to debulking.
- Just like the nonfunctional endocrine tumors, the liver is the **MC** site of metastases.
- 5-FU and Streptozocin work well in all the functional endocrine tumors.

- **Insulinomas** are the **MC** islet cell tumor of the pancreas.
- Symptoms include **Whipple's triad** (hypoglycemia, symptoms of hypoglycemia, and relief of symptoms with glucose).
- Most of these are **benign**, and occur evenly throughout the pancreas.
- Diagnosis is made with an **insulin to glucose ratio** of >0.4 and increased C-peptide levels.
- Treatment is resection.
- If there are metastases, give chemo (5-FU and Streptozocin).

- **Gastrinomas** (ZES) are **MCly** spontaneous, and are associated with **MEN syndrome type 1** in about 25% of cases.
- In MEN 1 patients, this is the **MC** type of pancreatic islet cell tumor.
- Unlike insulinomas which were benign and widespread throughout the pancreas, half of all gastrinomas are **malignant**, and most occur at the pancreatic head region.
- Symptoms include ulcers and diarrhea. The diarrhea here improves with H_2-blockers.
- A **serum gastrin level** in the 1000s is diagnostic.
- With a **secretin test**, normally serum gastrin levels decrease, but in gastrinomas it stays elevated at levels >200.
- Treatment is resection. Since half of these are **malignant**, resect all suspicious nodes.
- If you can't find the tumor during surgery, need to look in the duodenum as well (duodenostomy), since some of these tumors are in the duodenum. If this is the case, resect the tumor, and do a primary closure, or do a Whipple's if there is extensive local involvement. Just be sure that the duodenal lesion is the primary lesion, and not a metastasis.
- **Somatostatin receptor scintigraphy** is the single best test for localizing gastrinomas.
- Chronic renal failure can also cause elevated serum gastrin levels due to the decreased renal clearance, but levels are not as high as with gastrinomas.

- **Somatostatinomas** are very rare.
- They can cause gallstones and steatorrhea (due to decreased gallbladder secretion), symptoms similar to those of DM (decreased pancreatic endocrine secretions), as well as decreased gastric HCl secretion (decreased gastrin).
- Most of these are **malignant**, and are **MCly** located in the head of the pancreas (like Gastrinomas).

- **Glucagonomas** have symptoms similar to DM, but also dermatitis (**necrolytic migratory erythema**).
- Diagnosis is with a **fasting glucagon level**.
- Most glucagonomas are **malignant**, and **MCly** located in the distal pancreas (unlike gastrinomas and somatostatinomas)
- Can use Zinc and F.A.'s to treat the skin rash.

- **VIPoma** is also known as "**Verner-Morrison syndrome**".
- Symptoms include watery diarrhea, hypokalemia (diarrhea loss), and decreased gastric HCl secretion.
- Diagnosis is made with **increased serum VIP levels**, and also just ruling out other causes of diarrhea.
- Most of these are **malignant** (like gastrinomas, glucagonomas, and somatostatinomas), and most occur distally (like glucagonomas).
- These can occur extrapancreatically (ex. in the thorax).

- The splenic vein is posterior and inferior to the splenic artery.

- The spleen is the largest producer of **IgM**, and serves as an antigen-processing center for Macrophages (due to interactions between Macrophages and Th-cells).

- It's made up of 85% **red pulp**, which act as a filter for aged/damaged RBC's, via "pitting" or "culling".
- Damaged RBC's will have Howell-Jolly bodies (nuclear remnants) and/or Heinz bodies (Hb).

- The **white pulp** has immunologic functions, and contains lymphocytes and macrophages.
- It's the major site for the clearance of bacteria that lack antibody recognition, and is also the site of removal of poorly opsonized bacteria, particles, and other cellular debris.

- **Tuftsin**, an opsonin which facilitates phagocytosis, is produced in the spleen.
- **Properdin**, which activates the complement pathway, is also produced in the spleen.

- **Hematopoiesis** occurs in the spleen before birth, and also in certain conditions like MDS.

- Accessory spleens are **MCly** found at the splenic hilum.

- ITP is the **MC** non-traumatic condition requiring a splenectomy.
- Be sure to give the splenectomy vaccines at least 10-14 days pre-operatively

- **ITP** is multifactorial (ex. drugs, viruses), and is due to **anti-platelet IgG**. The spleen in ITP is normal.
- In kids, it usually resolves spontaneously. Otherwise can try steroids (first-line treatment), plasmapheresis, or gamma-globulin.
- If medical management fails, then a splenectomy is required, to remove the site of IgG production as well as the source of phagocytosis/removal of platelets.
- Preoperatively, when an urgent splenectomy is required for ITP, or in cases where steroids can't be used (like in pregnancy), gamma-globulins should be given to increase platelet count by temporarily reducing platelet destruction.
- Also have platelets on-hand during surgery just in case there is thrombocytopenic bleeding.

- **TTP** is also multifactorial (ex. infections, inflammation, auto-immune), and is due to loss of platelet inhibition, leading to thrombosis and infarction, and hence platelet consumption and profound thrombocytopenia.
- It presents with mental status change, renal dysfunction, and fever (neither of which are present in ITP).
- Most of these respond to medical therapy consisting of plasmapheresis (first-line treatment), and also steroids and ASA (to prevent thrombosis).
- Death in TTP is usually due to intracerebral hemorrhage or acute renal failure.

- **Post-splenectomy sepsis syndrome** (PSSS) has a 0.1% overall risk of occurring, and a slightly higher risk in children.
- It usually occurs within 2 years of the splenectomy.
- It's due to the specific lack of immunity against **encapsulated bacteria** (Streptococcus, Haemophilus, and Neisseria).
- Streptococcus, Haemophilus, and Neisseria are therefore the **MC** infectious organisms post-splenectomy.
- Can prevent PSSS by waiting until at least 5 years of age before doing a splenectomy, to allow for vaccinations, and proper antibody formation.

- Splenectomy results in pancytosis.
- Give ASA if platelets are >1,000,000.

- **Hemangiomas** (**benign**) are the **MC** splenic tumor. Surgery is only required if they are symptomatic.
- **Non-Hodgkin's lymphoma** is the **MC malignant** splenic tumor.

- For **splenic cysts**, do surgery only if they're symptomatic or >10cm in size.

- **Hypersplenism** results in pancytopenia.
- By definition, hypersplenism needs to have an appropriate hematopoietic response by the bone marrow, because otherwise the pancytopenia is due to a bone marrow problem.
- **Primary hypersplenism** is rare, so rule out other causes. True primary hypersplenism is an indication to do a splenectomy.
- **Secondary hypersplenism** is **MCly** associated with: portal hypertension/CHF, malignancy (leukemia), chronic inflammatory diseases (SLE, sarcoidosis), myeloproliferative diseases, amyloidosis, and AIDS.
- Do a splenectomy in secondary hypersplenism only if it is associated with leukemia/lymphoma, sarcoidosis, or if the portal HTN is due to a splenic vein thrombosis.

- **Felty's syndrome** is R.A., hepatomegaly, and splenomegaly. A splenectomy is only required if it's symptomatic.

- **Gaucher's disease** is a lipid metabolism disorder, and can cause splenomegaly.
- A partial splenectomy may be effective in treating Gaucher's disease.

- **Spherocytosis** is the **MC congenital** hemolytic anemia requiring a splenectomy.
- It is due to a deficiency in the membrane protein **Spectrin**.
- Treatment is not only with a splenectomy (after >5 years old), but also a cholecystectomy, since most patients with spherocytosis will have pigmented stones as a result of elevated bilirubin levels from hemolyzed RBC's.
- **Protein 4.1 deficiency** causes Elliptocytosis since it is involved in the spectrin-actin complex of RBC membrane's.

- **Pyruvate Kinase deficiency** results in congential hemolytic anemia, due to altered glucose metabolism.
- It is the **MC** congenital hemolytic anemia not involving the RBC membrane, requiring a splenectomy.
- Doing a splenectomy in pyruvate kinase deficiency prolongs the RBC's life.

- Hemolytic anemias due to warm antibodies require a Splenectomy.

- **Beta-thalassemia** (the **MC** type of thalassemia) may require a splenectomy to decrease hemolysis and symptoms, especially since most causes of β-thalassemia major die in their teens due to hemosiderosis.

- **G6PD deficiency** and **Sickle Cell** are two causes of hemolytic anemia where a splenectomy is not indicated.

- **Hairy Cell leukemia** requires splenectomy as well as Interferon-γ.

- **Splenic artery aneurysms** (discussed in more detail in the *Vascular Surgery* chapter), are the **MC** type of visceral aneurysm, and carry the lowest risk of rupture.
- They only require repair if they are symptomatic, or if it is a pregnant/child-bearing age woman because of the high rate of rupture during pregnancy (usually in the 3rd trimester when the uterus is high enough to put pressure on the spleen).

GI - SMALL BOWEL

- The 2nd and 3rd portions of the duodenum are retroperitoneal
- The 3rd and 4th portions pass anterior to the aorta, but posterior to the SMA.

- The **jejunum** is ~100cm long, and has long vasa recta.
- Absorption of most nutrients occurs in the Jejunum, except for iron (absorbed in the duodenum), and vitamin B12, bile acids and folate (absorbed in the ileum).

- The **ileum** is ~150cm long, and has short vasa recta.
- Absorption of vitamin B12, bile acids, and folate occurs in the ileum.
- Complications of an **ileectomy** therefore include: decreased absorption of vitamin B12/folate (**anemia**), decreased absorption of bile salts (**steatorrhea** and **gallstones**), as well as too much bile getting into the colon, thereby increasing the permeability to oxalate, and sequestering calcium (**kidney stones**).

- The small bowel wall contains the enzymes maltase, sucrase, and lactase

- The cell types in the small bowel include **goblet cells** (secrete mucin), **paneth cells** (secrete granules/ enzymes), **enterochromaffin cells** (release hormones/enzymes), **Brunner's glands** (release alkaline fluid), and **M cells** (antigen-presenting cells).

- **Motilin** is the most important hormone in migratory motor complexes (MMC's).
- Phase 1 MMC is rest, phase 2 MMC is intermittent spikes, phase 3 MMC is maximum spike activity superimposed on the slow waves, causing regular, strong, contractions, and phase 4 MMC is deceleration.
- This entire cycle lasts ~2 hours long.
- MMC's are only present during a fasting state, and therefore play no role postprandially. Rather, they rid the bowel of residual food, secretions, and dead cells during fasting.

- **Fat and cholesterol** are broken down in the small bowel by cholesterol esterase, phospholipase A_2, lipase, and bile salts.
- These are converted to F.A.'s and monoglycerides, which in turn form micelles.
- Long-chain F.A.'s are taken up by enterocytes, where they are re-made into TG's, and are released into the lymphatics as chylomicrons.
- Chylomicrons are therefore about 90% TG's.
- Short and medium-chain F.A.'s go straight into the portal venous system.

- 95% of **bile salts** are reabsorbed (by both passive and active transport), and almost entirely in the ileum.
- Resection of the terminal ileum can therefore predispose to gallstone formation, due to the malabsorption of bile.
- The **primary bile acids** are **cholic acid** and **chenodeoxycholic acid**.
- The **secondary bile acids** (after bacteria act on them) include **deoxycholic acid** and **lithocholic acid**.

- **Conjugated bilirubin** is only absorbed by the terminal ileum, but can also be deconjugated by bacteria, and absorbed in the colon.

- **Short-gut syndrome** is diagnosed based on symptoms, not based on the length of the remaining bowel.
- Complications include loss of water, electrolytes, fat, and vitamin B12.
- Can check for fat in stool using a **Sudan red stain**.
- **Schilling test** checks radiolabeled vitamin B12 in the urine, and can therefore assess vitamin B12 absorption.

- **Steatorrhea** can be caused by gastric acid hypersecretion, because the acidity will increase GI motility and hence interfere with fat absorption.

- Risk factors for **fistulas** include Foreign bodies, Radiation, IBD, Epithelialization, Neoplasm, Distal obstruction, and Sepsis/infection.
- Proximal (duodenum, proximal jejunum) fistulas have a high output and are more likely not to heal with conservative management.
- Otherwise most fistulas do heal spontaneously, treated only with conservative management (i.e. TPN, NGT, stoma bag).
- In case of fever in a patient with a fistula, check for an abscess (CT, sinogram, upper GI...)
- A surgical option for an enterocutaneous fistula is segmental resection of the bowel segment containing the fistula, and primary anastomosis.

- Without any previous adominal surgeries, small bowel obstruction is **MCly** due to a hernia, and large bowel obstruction is **MCly** due to cancer.
- With any previous abdominal surgery, small bowel obstruction is **MCly** due to adhesions, but large bowel obstruction is still **MCly** due to cancer.
- Air seen in obstruction is due to swallowed air.
- Surgery is indicated if there is fever, peritoneal signs, or increasing WBC.
- Otherwise most heal with conservative management: NG tube, NPO, and IV fluids.

- **Meckel's diverticulum** is a true diverticulum, and is due to a remnant omphalomesenteric duct.
- In patients <2 years old, Meckel's diverticulum is the culprit in half the cases of painless lower GI bleeds.
- Pancreatic tissue is the **MC** tissue type found in Meckel's, but Gastric mucosa is the **MC** tissue in Meckel's to be symptomatic.
- In adults, it typically presents as an obstruction.
- Diagnosis is made with a **Meckel's scan**, and treatment is a diverticulectomy.
- If the lumen of the diverticulum is large or if gastric mucosa involves the base of the diverticulum, a segmental bowel resection is required.

- **Duodenal diverticula** can be treated non-surgically with simple observation, unless they are problematic.

- Surgery is the **MCC** of **ileus**.
- Other causes of ileus include electrolyte abnormalities, peritonitis, ischemia, and trauma.
- In ileus, the GI dilation is uniform throughout the GI tract. In obstruction, the distal bowel is decompressed, and only the proximal bowel is dilated.

Crohn's disease:
- Extraintestinal manifestations of Crohn's include joint pains, ocular problems, anemia from folate/B12 malabsorption, and growth failure.
- Crohn's has **transmural** involvement, and is **segmental**.
- There can be deep **ulcers**, creeping fat, and **fistulas**.
- The **anus** is commonly involved.

- The terminal ileum is the **MCly** involved segment of bowel, and is also the **MC** site of initial presentation.

- A colonoscopy with biopsies can often help make the diagnosis.

- Treatment is 5-ASA, Sulfasalazine, steroids, immunosuppressants (these only give symptomatic relief though, nothing 'cures' it, not even surgery).
- Infliximab (*Remicade*, a TNF-α blocker) helps with fistulas.
- NPO with TPN can help flare-ups and help fistulas close.

- Surgery is usually not indicated, as most of the complications can be treated medically.
- Surgery may help in certain cases, such as distal ileum involvement, or colon/rectal involvement.

- Anal fissures in Crohn's are not treated with a lateral sphincteroplasty, as they are in non-Crohn's fissures (discussed in more detail in the *Anorectal* chapter)

- If see Crohn's during an appendectomy, take the appendix out only if the cecum is not affected with Crohn's.

- Stricturoplasty is only indicated if there are multiple strictures.

- There is an increased risk of small bowel malignancy in Crohn's disease.

Carcinoid:

- Serotonin is made by "**Kulchitsky cells**", also known as **enterochromaffin cells**, which are a type of amine precursor decarboxylase (APUD) cells.

- The appendix is the **MC** location for a carcinoid, followed by the ileum, and then the rectum.
- Ileal carcinoids are **MCly** metastatic, and are more likely to have multiple primaries, as well as a second, unrelated cancer elsewhere.

- In carcinoid syndrome, getting symptoms means the tumor has already metastasized to the liver.
- Symptoms include: intermittent flushing (treat with α-blockers), diarrhea (due to mesenteric vasoconstriction and fibrosis), and asthma-symptoms (bronchospasms).

- By using up all the Trp to make Serotonin, carcinoid syndrome can cause a Trp deficiency.
- Since Niacin is also made from Trp, carcinoid syndrome can therefore cause a Niacin deficiency.

- Diagnosis can be made by measuring a 24 hour urine **5-HIAA** level (breakdown product of Serotonin).
- Some fruits have metabolites that can give a falsely elevated 5-HIAA.

- Can then do a CT scan to identify the tumor. If the primary tumor is not seen on a CT scan, an **Octreotide scan** can help localize the tumor.

- All patients with a carcinoid tumor need an abdominal exploration.

- If the primary is in the appendix, and the tumor is <2cm, can simply do an appendectomy.
- If the tumor is >2 cm, we need more than just an appendectomy because of the potential for metastases. Treatment is therefore a right hemicolectomy.

- If the primary is in the small bowel, and the tumor is <1 cm with no node involvement, can treat with a segmental resection.
- If the tumor is >1 cm, there is node involvement, or multiple primaries, then need a wide excision of the bowel as well as the mesentery.

- With a primary elsewhere (ex. rectum), treat like any other tumor: resection and lymphadenectomy.

- With unresectable disease, treat with chemotherapy.

Small bowel neoplasms:

- Benign small bowel tumors are rare, yet they are still more common than malignant small bowel tumors.
- **Leiomyomas** are the **MC benign** small bowel tumors, followed by Adenomas.

- **"Peutz-Jeghers syndrome"** (autosomal dominant inheritance) is characterized by jejunal and ileal hamartomas and mucus membrane/skin melanotic pigmentation.
- It carries an increased risk of colon Ca, as well as lipomas, hemangiomas, and neurogenic tumors.

- **AdenoCa** is the **MC malignant** small bowel tumor.
- It **MCly** affects the duodenum.
- Treatment is resection, unless it involves the 2nd portion of the duodenum, in which case a Whipple's procedure is required.
- FAP and Gardner's syndrome increase the risk of small bowel AdenoCa.

- **Leiomyosarcoma** of the small bowel is usually in the jejunum or ileum.
- >5 mitoses per HPF differentiates Leiomyosarcomas from benign Leiomyomas.
- Treatment is resection.

- Small bowel **Lymphoma** is usually in the ileum, and is associated with Crohn's, SLE, AIDS, Wegener's and Celiac sprue.
- Treatment is en bloc resection with node resection, as well as chemo / radiation.
- Most of these are non-Hodgkin's.

Stomas:

- The best treatment for parastomal hernias is repositioning of the stoma.
- Candida is the **MC** stomal infection.
- Ischemia is the **MCC** of stoma stenosis.
- Crohn's disease is the **MCC** of fistula formation near a stoma site.
- A **"diversion colitis"** is inflammation of the blind distal bowel stump, due to the diversion of stool. It's due to a deficiency in short-chain fatty acids in the distal bowel, since the large bowel uses small-chain F.A.'s for nutrition.
- Can therefore treat diversion colitis with short-chain F.A. enemas.

Appendix:

- Patients with appendicitis can have a normal WBC count.
- The portion of the appendix most likely to perforate is the midpoint, on the antimesenteric side.

- In kids, lymphoid hyperplasia is the **MCC** of appendicitis.
- In adults, a fecalith is the **MCC**.
- In both cases, the pathophysiology is the same: obstruction of the appendiceal lumen resulting in distention, venous congestions and/or thrombosis, and ultimately ischemia/necrosis.

- If there is a walled-off perforated appendix, treatment is percutaneous drainage and a delayed appendectomy when symptoms are improving.

- Kids and elderly are more likely to rupture, because they typically present later in the course of the illness.

- During pregnancy, appendicitis is the **MCC** of acute abdominal pain in the 1st trimester.
- Overall, it's more likely to occur in the 2nd semester, where it is not the most common cause of abdominal pain.
- It's most likely to perforate in the 3rd semester. If this happens, there is a 35% risk of fetal death.
- Because the appendix can move around during pregnancy, need to make the incision where the patient is having pain. In the 3rd trimester, this might even be in the RUQ.

- The colon absorbs Na$^+$ and water, and secretes K$^+$.
- It has 4 layers: mucosa (contains muscularis mucosa), submucosa, muscularis propria, and serosa
- The ascending, descending, and sigmoid colons are all retroperitoneal

- The marginal artery runs along the colon (connecting the SMA to the IMA). The **"arc of Riolan"** is the specific portion of the marginal artery connecting the middle colic (branch off SMA) to the left colic (branch off IMA).
- **"Griffith's point"** is the watershed area at the splenic flexure.
- **"Sudak's point"** is the watershed area at the rectum.

- 80% of the blood supply to the colon goes to the inner layers (mucosa and submucosa).

- The rectum is supplied by the superior rectal artery (off the IMA), the middle rectal artery (off the internal iliac), and the inferior rectal (off the internal pudendal).

- The IMV drains into the splenic vein.
- Middle rectal vein, even though is a branch off the internal iliac, drains into the IMV.
- Inferior rectal vein drains into the internal iliac veins.

- In terms of lymphatics, the entire rectum drains into IMA nodes, though the lower rectum also drains into internal iliac nodes.

- The **external anal sphincter** (puborectalis muscle) is under voluntary control. It's innervated by the inferior rectal branch of the internal pudendal nerve.
- The **internal anal sphincter** is under involuntary control. It's the continuation of the circular bands of colonic smooth muscle, and it's normally contracted.

- Meissner's plexus is the inner nerve plexus (motor).
- Auerbach's is the outer nerve plexus (secretions).
- Crypts of Lieberkühn are mucus-secreting goblet cells.

- The rectum is 5-15 cm from the anal verge.

- **"Denonvilliers fascia"** is anterior to the rectum (rectovesicular/rectovaginal fascia).
- **"Waldeyer's fascia"** is posterior to the rectum (retrosacral fascia).

- Vitamin C, antacids, and cimetidine can all give false-positive guaiac tests.

- **Sigmoid volvulus** (**MC** type of colonic volvulus) is associated with high-fiber diets, chronic constipation, laxative abuse, and also psychiatric/institutionalized patients.
- Patients present with signs of large bowel obstruction and abdominal pain.
- Diagnosis can usually be made with a plain film, though may also use a barium enema (though avoid barium enemas if there are peritoneal signs, or signs of a possible perforation).
- If there are peritoneal signs, need surgery. Otherwise treatment is colonoscopic decompression.
- Even with successful decompression, a sigmoidectomy should still be done electively since half of these will recur.

- **Cecal volvulus** is less common than sigmoid volvulus.
- It is often not decompressable with colonoscopy, and hence needs surgical treatment with a hemicolectomy.
- Can do a cecopexy if the patient is a poor surgical candidate.

Colorectal polyps:

- The **MC** type of polyps are hyperplastic (adenomatous) polyps. These have no cancer risk.
- **Tubular adenomas** are the **MC** neoplastic intestinal polyps.
- **Villous adenomas**, though less common, are more likely to be cancerous (invasive/malignant).
- If can't resect a polyp endoscopically, need to do a segmental resection.
- Invasion through the basement membrane is when a tumor has gone passed the mucosa and into the submucosa.
- A polyp resection of a T1 lesion (invasion to the basement membrane) is adequate if the margins are at least 2mm, and if there's no vascular/lymphatic invasion. Otherwise would need a resection.

- With regards to **villous adenomas**, their size is directly related to their risk of being cancer: >4 cm villous adenoma is cancer 90% of the time.
- With villous adenomas in the rectum, the first step in management is to do a transanal excisional biopsy, due to the high risk of sampling error seen with an endoscopic biopsy.
- This should include adequate margins due to the high risk of recurrence if inadequate excision is performed, and should also include tattooing of the mucosa to facilitate future/follow-up colonoscopic examination.
- If it covers a large portion of the surface of the rectum, need to do a rectal resection with a coloanal anastomoses.
- Villous adenomas of the small bowel are rare, but can occur, **MCly** in the duodenum.

- **Rectal polyps** can secrete water and electrolytes like potassium. This causes diarrhea and hypokalemia, because the distal colon and rectum do not reabsorb potassium.

- T1 is invasion into the basement membrane. T2 is into the muscularis propria. T3 is into the serosa. T4 is passed the serosa and into the peritoneal cavity or adjacent organs/structures.
- Stage 1 is T1-2, N0, M0. Stage 2 is T3-4, N0, M0. Stage 3 is any N1. Stage 4 is any M1.

- For an average person, screening should start at 50, followed by a colonoscopy every 10 years.
- With FAP, screening should start at 10, with annual sigmoidoscopies.
- With HNPCC, screening should start at 20.

- With a polyp resection, need follow-up colonoscopy 5 years later.
- With a colon resection for colorectal cancer, need follow-up colonoscopy within 1 year.

- **Juvenile polyposes** are hamartomatous polyps.
- **"Peutz-Jeghers syndrome"** is hamartomatous polyps, but with mucosal dark pigmentation.
- **"Cronkite-Canada syndrome"** is hamartomatous polyps, but associated with nail atrophy, alopecia, and skin pigmentation.
- None of these are malignant, but patients with these are at higher risk of getting Colorectal Ca.

Colorectal Cancer:

- This is the 2nd leading cause of Cancer-related death (lung is **MC**).
- A diet high in fats is believed to play a role, by promoting O_2-radical formation.
- There is also an association with Clostridium Septicum.

- The genes involved are APC, DCC, p53, MSH-2, and k-ras.

- The sigmoid colon is the **MC** site of a primary colon Ca.

- The prognosis is worst if the patient is young, symptomatic, if it's a rectosigmoid location, if there is blood/lymphatic invasion, or if there is an elevated CEA.
- Prognosis is improved if there is lymphocytic infiltration.
- The most important prognostic factor is the lymph node status.

- The liver is the **MC** site of metastasis (via the portal vein), followed by the lungs (via the iliac vein).
- Solitary liver/lung metastases should be resected, though even with metastasis resection, the overall mortality rate is still high.
- This is worse if there is >3 metastases, metastases >5cm, or if CEA is >200.
- Resection of liver metastases is not indicated if there is systemic metastasis or carcinomatosis.

- Batson's plexus (valveless vein plexus) allows for direct metastases of rectal Ca to the spine.

- Intraoperative U/S is the best method of picking up intrahepatic metastases.

- **Abdominoperineal resection** (APR) is excision of the sigmoid colon, rectum and anal canal. It therefore results in a permanent colostomy.
- It is only indicated for malignant/invasive lesions of the lower rectum.
- If the lesion is >2cm above the levator ani, can get away with a low anterior resection, leaving the anus/perineum intact.
- The disruption in the nerve supply makes for a high rate of impotence (in men) and also bladder dysfunction.
- If there are unresectable metastases elsewhere, APR is not indicated since it will not be curative, unless it's solely for symptomatic reasons (obstruction, bleeding, pain, etc).

- In colon Ca: Stage 3 and 4 (any N1 and M1 respectively), should get chemo.
- In rectal Ca: Stage 2 (T3-4, N0, M0) and above should get chemo and radiation.
- Low rectal Ca, even if it's just T2, requires an APR. (other indications for APR in rectal Ca include lesions >4 cm, >⅓ in circumference or >6 cm from the dendate line)

- 20% of patients with colorectal cancer will have recurrence.
- Half of these will be in the first 6 months and almost all of them by 3 years. This is why a follow-up colonoscopy is recommended within 1 year.
- Many patients have other primary Colon tumors as well.

Familial Adenomatous Polyposis (FAP):

- FAP has an autosomal dominant inheritance pattern.
- It is associated with the APC gene, and always causes cancer by age 40.
- 20% of these are due to a spontaneous gene mutations, with no family history.
- Polyps here are not present at birth, but start in puberty. Endoscopic screening therefore starts at 10 years of age.
- Sigmoidoscopy suffices, since we are looking for any polyps, and FAP is usually extensive enough to affect the sigmoid colon as well.
- Patients with FAP need a prophylactic colectomy by age 20. If the rectum is retained, frequent proctoscopic exams are required.
- Gastric and duodenal polyps/adenomas are common in FAP as well, so need to do upper endoscopies regularly after 30 years old.
- Following a colectomy, the **MCC** of death here is a duodenal tumor involving the ampulla.
- Gardner's syndrome is FAP with Desmoid tumors/Osteomas.
- Turcot's syndrome is FAP with brain tumors.

Lynch Syndrome:

- **"Lynch Syndrome"** (HNPCC) has an autosomal dominant inheritance pattern, and is associated with the DNA mismatch repair genes MLH1 and MSH2.
- Type I only carries a risk of developing Colon Ca. Type II also carries a risk of developing ovarian, endometrial, bladder and stomach Ca.
- Diagnosis requires at least three 1st-degree relatives over 2 generations, one of whom had cancer before 50 years old.
- Endoscopic surveillance is required starting at 20 years old.
- Women with HNPCC require frequent endometrial biopsies due to the risk of endometrial Ca. Consider a

TAH/BSO if the woman no longer wishes to become pregnant.

Ulcerative Colitis (U.C.):

- Ulcerative Colitis involves the mucosa and submucosa only.
- Unlike in Crohn's, strictures, fistulas, and granulomas in U.C. are unlikely.
- The rectum is usually involved here, but the anus is spared.
- U.C. always presents with bleeding, and this is due to mucosal friability.

- Medical treatment includes 5-ASA, sulfasalazine, steroids and immunosuppressants.
- Toxic megacolon presents with fever, and a dilated colon. Treatment is with IV fluids, NPO, NG tube, steroids, and antibiotics. If doesn't help, surgery is required.

- Perforation in U.C. is more common in the transverse colon, whereas in Crohn's it was most common in the distal ileum

- Need colonoscopies starting at 8-10 years after diagnosis due to the increased risk of Colon Ca.
- Long-standing (>10 years) disease may even warrant a prophylactic colectomy to prevent Ca.
- As part of the colectomy here, can do an ileoanal anastomosis with a J-pouch (which we can't do with Crohn's).
- Need a diverting ileostomy for 6-8 weeks while the J-pouch heals.
- The ileoanal anastomosis can fail due to cancer or refractory inflammation, causing leak/sepsis.

- Extraintestinal manifestations of U.C. include: ocular problems, arthritis, anemia, primary sclerosing cholangitis, pyoderma gangrenosum, DVT's, and ankylosing spondylitis.
- As a rule of thumb, the presence of extraintestinal manifestations in U.C. is an indication to do a colectomy.

Carcinoid:

- Carcinoid is **MC** in the appendix, followed by the Ileum, and then the rectum.
- With rectal carcinoid, the size of the rectal carcinoid correlates with malignancy risk (most rectal carcinoid tumors >2 cm have liver metastases and local lymph node involvement).
- So rectal carcinoid tumors >2 cm, or those that invade the muscularis propria, will need to be resected.
- If it's a high-rectal lesion, may be able to do an anterior resection, otherwise will need an APR.
- Rectal carcinoid tumors <2 cm can be treated with a transanal excision or endoscopic excision.
- (Cardinoid syndrome is discussed in more detail in the *Small Bowel* chapter)

Miscellaneous:

- **Large bowel obstruction** is **MCly** due to cancer, followed by diverticulitis.
- Large bowel obstruction leading to perforation is most likely in the cecum.

- **Ogilvie's syndrome** is associated with opiates, inactivity, and recent surgery/stress/infection/trauma.
- Treatment is NPO and correcting electrolyte abnormalities.
- Can try colonoscopic decompression, or Neostigmine to stimulate the colon.

- **Amebic colitis** is due to Entamoeba Histolytica.
- Risk factors include travel to exotic countries and alcohol abuse.
- It presents with fever, cramps, and frequent bowel movements.
- Diagnose by checking serum anti-amebic antibodies, and treat with Metronidazole.

- **Actinomyces MCly** affects the cecum, and can lead to abscess formation, fistulas, and granulomas.
- Treat with PCN or Tetracycline, and drain if there is an abscess.

- **Lymphogranuloma Venereum** in the colon/rectum is due to Chlamydia (STD) as a result of anal sex.

- It can cause proctitis, tenesmus, and GI bleeding.
- Treat with Doxycycline.

- **Diverticula** occur due to increased intraluminal pressure, in locations where arteries enter the muscular wall.
- Circular muscles adjacent to diverticula typically thicken, causing luminal narrowing in those regions.
- Although left-sided diverticula are more common overall, bleeding diverticula are more common with right-sided diverticula.

- **Diverticulosis** is the **MCC** of lower GI bleeding, but in any case of diverticulosis we still need to rule out Cancer.
- Bleeding here usually stops spontaneously.
- Management first requires resuscitation. If the patient responds to resuscitation, do a colonoscopy or an angiogram.
- If the patient is unresponsive to resuscitation, need surgery.
- Recurrent diverticular bleeding warrants a resection of the affected segment of bowel.

- **Diverticulitis** is due to perforation of a diverticulum, resulting in fecal contamination.
- Diagnosis is made with a CT scan. Avoid scoping or barium enemas in diverticulitis.
- Eventually, these patients will need a barium enema to rule out cancer as the cause of the perforation.
- "Complicated diverticulitis" (fever, white count, obstruction, peritoneal signs, non-drainable abscess) requires surgery. Otherwise can treat with antibiotics, IV fluids, and NPO.
- The **MC** complication in diverticulitis is abscess formation, which requires percutaneous drainage.
- If a right-sided diverticulitis is found during an appendectomy, need to do a right hemicolectomy.

- In **lower GI bleed**, stool guaiac can stay positive for up to 3 weeks after a bleed.
- Azotemia after a GI bleed is not due to renal insufficiency, but rather due to urea production by gut bacteria acting on the intraluminal blood.
- Bleeding must be >0.5 cc/min for an arteriography to pick it up.

- **Angiodysplasia** bleeds are caused by venous bleeding (whereas diverticular bleeds are arterial).
- Angiodysplasia is associated with aortic stenosis.

- Abdominal pain with bright red lower GI bleeding can be **ischemic colitis**.
- Common causes of ischemic colitis include mesenteric emboli, septic shock, and cardiogenic shock (MI).
- Emboli to the mesenteric vessels are **MCly** from the heart.
- The splenic flexure (Griffith's point) is the most vulnerable to low-flow states.
- Diagnosis can be made with endoscopy (pale, exudative mucosa).
- If there are peritoneal signs, do not do colonoscopy, but rather go straight to the OR.

- **Pseudomembranous colitis** can occur up to 3 weeks after antibiotic therapy.
- A key finding here is PMN inflammation of the mucosa and submucosa.

- Neutrophilic Typhlitis (enterocolitis) occurs post-chemo, as a result of leukopenia.

- TB enteritis can present like Crohn's disease (stricture/stenosis).
- Treatment is like any other case of TB.

- Trypanosoma Cruzi (the cause of Chaga's disease) can cause megacolon.

GI - ANORECTAL

- The venous drainage of the anus is the **internal hemorrhoid plexus** above the dentate line, and **external hemorrhoid plexus** below the dentate line.
- The dentate line (also called pectinate line) divides the upper 2/3 and the lower 1/3 of the anal canal.

- **External hemorrhoids** are painful when they thrombus.   This is because distal to the dentate line, the hemorrhoids are covered with squamous epithelium and have pain receptors.

- **Internal hemorrhoids** are divided into primary (slide below the dentate line with straining), secondary (prolapse, but reduces spontaneously), tertiary (prolapse that needs manual reduction), and quaternary (non-reducible).

- Treatment of hemorrhoids is stool softening, and sitz baths.
- Indications for surgery include recurrent bleeding, recurrent thrombosis, or quaternary internal hemorrhoids.

- **Rectal prolapse** occurs from laxity of the anal sphincter, like with pudendal nerve neuropathy.
- Chronic diarrhea, pregnancy, straining, and a redundant sigmoid colon are all risk factors for rectal prolapse.
- By definition, a rectal prolapse involves all layers of the rectum.
- Treatment is stool softening (high-fiber diet, etc). Can also do a rectopexy, or a transanal rectosigmoidectomy if there is lots of redundant colon.

- 90% of **anal fissures** are in the posterior midline, and will present with pain and bleeding after defecation.
- If the fissure is lateral or recurrent, consider Crohn's or U.C. as the cause of the fissure.
- Chronically, it can cause thickening of the mucus membrane (called an anal skin tag or sentinel pile).
- Treatment is medical; sitz baths, lidocaine jelly, and stool softening.
- Can consider incising the internal rectal sphincter laterally (lateral internal sphincterotomy), to relieve pressure during defecation.
- Do not do surgery if the fissures are due to Crohn's or U.C.

- In terms of **anorectal abscesses**, perianal, intersphincteric, and ischiorectal abscess can be drained percutaneously, since they are all below the levator ani muscles.
- Of these three, only intersphincteric and ischiorectal abscesses can form horseshoe abscesses, since they are within the sphincter muscles (intersphincteric) or lateral to the sphincter muscles (ischiorectal).
- Supralevator abscesses (above the levator ani muscles), need to be drained transrectally.
- Antibiotics are only required if there is an overlying cellulitis, or if the patient has DM or is immunocompromised.

- With **anal fistulas**, treatment is not necessarily to excise the tract, but rather just cover the primary opening with a rectal advancement flap.
- **"Goodsall's rule"** dictates that anterior fistulas come straight up from the rectum, whereas posterior fistulas have a curved track from the rectum.

- **Simple rectovaginal fistulas** are caused by infections or OB/GYN trauma.
- Treat these transanally with a rectal mucosa flap, though many OB/GYN-induced rectovaginal fistulas heal spontaneously.

- **Complex rectovaginal fistulas** are due to IBD, radiation, or cancers.
- Treat these with an abdominal approach, by resecting the fistula, and placing a colostomy.

- If **anal incontinence** is due to trauma (like with childbirth), the problem is likely a lax and fibrotic anterior external sphincter.
- Treat with an overlapping anal sphincteroplasty, where the external anal sphincter anteriorly is wrapped around the anus.

- In AIDS patients, look anorectally for **HSV** (**MCC** of rectal ulcer in AIDS patients), **Kaposi's sarcoma** (**MC** cancer overall in AIDS patients, though **MCly** in the oropharynx), and **CMV**.
- All of these can present with ulcers, and all need biopsies to rule out cancer.

Anal cancer:

- Anal cancer is associated with HPV and radiation.

- Symptoms include itching and/or bleeding.

- First line treatment of **anal canal SCC** is chemo and radiation, not surgery.
- If there is adenopathy (like in the inguinal lymph nodes), need to get a FNA. If FNA is positive for anal cancer, extend the radiation to cover the inguinal lymph nodes.
- ~80% of anal cancers get cured. If it persists or recurs, an abdominoperineal resection is required.

- In cases of an **anal canal adenoCa**, need an abdominoperineal resection, as well as chemo / radiation.

- **Anal verge** lesions are **SCC**.
- These are slow-growing, and have a better prognosis than those in the anal canal.
- Treatment is a local excision if the lesion is <3cm, or an abdominoperineal resection if the lesion is >3cm.

- **Anal melanoma** is the 3rd **MC** site for a melanoma (skin is MC, eyes are second MC).
- Death is **MCly** due to metastases to the liver/lungs.
- **MC** symptom is rectal bleeding.

- "**Bowen's disease**" is an intraepidermal form of SCC.
- Treatment is a wide local excision, but since this is highly **malignant**, need to check for other internal cancers.

HERNIAS AND ABDOMEN

- The internal oblique muscle forms the cremasteric muscles.
- The transversalis muscle forms the inguinal canal floor.

- The **Lacunar ligament** is where the inguinal ligament splays out to insert into the pubis.
- **Cooper's ligament** is an extension of this lacunar ligament that runs on the pectineal line (a ridge on the superior ramus of the pubic bone), which is why it's also known as the pectineal ligament.

- The **conjoined tendon** is made up of the aponeurosis of the internal abdominal oblique muscle and the transversalis abdominal muscles.

- Direct hernias have a lower risk of incarceration, but a higher risk of recurrence.

- When there is a direct and indirect hernia, it's called a "**Pantaloon hernia**".

- Can get an **inguinal sliding hernia**, where in males the sigmoid or cecum slides down, or in females, the ovaries or fallopian tubes slides down.
- To repair an inguinal sliding ovarian hernia in females, need to resect the round ligament, because it's likely what pulled it into the canal.

- The common open method with an overlay mesh is the **Lichtenstein repair**.
- **Bassini repair** is closing the defect by pulling the transversalis fascia and conjoined tendon (superior/medial) to the edge of the inguinal ligament (inferior).
- **McVay repair** is closing the defect by pulling the transversalis fascia and conjoined tendon (superior/medial) to Cooper's ligament.

- **Urinary retention** is the **MC early** complication of hernia repairs.
- In a McVay repair, can get femoral vein constriction resulting in post-op DVT.

- **Testicular atrophy** can occur after hernia repairs, due to blood vessel disruption secondary to dissection of the distal component of the hernia sac.

- **Chronic pain** after hernia repairs is usually due to compression of the **ilioinguinal nerve** (this runs anterior to the structures).
- **Paresthesias** to the groin, scrotum, and upper thigh, as well as loss of the cremasteric reflex, are due to damage to the genital branch of the **genitofemoral nerve**. (this runs deeper in the structures)

- Cord lipomas need to be resected.

- **Femoral hernias** are more common in females, and have a high risk of incarceration (may need to divide the inguinal ligament to reduce the bowel).

- **Spigelian hernia** is at the lateral border of the rectus muscle (through the linea semilunaris).
- **Petit's hernia** is at the inferior lumbar area, through the external oblique muscles and/or latissimus muscles.
- **Grynfeltt's hernia** is at the superior lumbar area, through the internal oblique muscles.
- **Littre's hernia** is a hernia involving Meckel's diverticulum.
- **Sciatic hernia** is through the greater sciatic foramen.
- **Obturator hernia** is through the obturator foramen. Look for inner thigh pain on internal rotation ("**Howship-Romberg sign**").

Abdomen:

- The posterior rectus sheath is absent below the semicircularis (arcuate line), since all three muscles pass anteriorly below this line.

- A rectus sheath hematoma is most common after trauma, as a result of epigastric vessel injury.
- Abdominal mass and pain in a rectus sheath hematoma are more prominent with abdominal flexion ("**Fothergill's sign**").
- Treatment is conservative. Surgery is required only if it's expanding.

- **Retroperitoneal fibrosis** can be caused by hypersensitivity to certain medications (ex. the anti-migraine medication Methylsergide).
- Symptoms are usually due to trapped ureters and lymphatic obstruction, and therefore an IVP is the most sensitive test.
- Treat with steroids, and surgery to free the ureters if renal function becomes compromised.

- **Retroperitoneal tumors** are usually **malignant**, and are **MCly** lymphomas, followed by liposarcomas.
- Retroperitoneal liposarcomas are usually not resectable and have a poor prognosis, with metastases **MCly** to the lungs.

- Most **mesenteric tumors** are cystic.
- Most solid mesenteric tumor are **benign**.
- The **malignant** types include liposarcomas and leiomyosarcomas. These usually occur closer to the root of the mesentery (whereas benign ones occur more commonly peripherally).

- **Omental tumors** are usually metastases from elsewhere, since primary omental tumors are rare.
- If you see it, simply resect it. An omentectomy therefore doesn't have a role, except for some cancers, like ovarian Ca.

- Most drugs cannot be removed with peritoneal dialysis, though Iron, Lead, Ammonia and Calcium can.
- Using a lot of hypertonic saline in the peritoneal cavity can shift volume into the peritoneum and cause hypotension.

- CO_2 pneumoperitoneum causes decreased renal flow, due to renal vein compression.
- CO_2 pneumoperitoneum also causes decreased venous return, which results in a decreased cardiac output, and hence a compensatory increase in HR, systemic vascular resistance, and pulmonary vascular resistance to compensate for the decrease in cardiac output.

- Gore-Tex (PTFE) graft does not allow fibroblast ingrowth, whereas Polypropylene graft does.

- **Type 1 error** is saying there is a difference when there is none.
- **Type 2 error** is saying there is no difference when there really is one.

- **P<0.05** rejects the null hypothesis (i.e. means there is a difference).

- If the 95% **confidence interval** includes the value 1, it is not significant.
- The further it is from the number 1, the strong the correlation; for example 0.1, or 9.

- **Case-control** is retrospective.
- The main limitations of retrospective studies include the inability to randomize the patients, inability to manipulate the variables, and a higher rate of false interpretations due to lots of confounding effects.

- **Cohort** is prospective.

- **Student's t-test** (compares mean values between 2 groups) and **ANOVA** (compares mean values between >2 groups) are quantitative.

- **Chi-squared** (compares qualitative values between 2 groups) and **Kaplan-Meyer** (estimate survival) are qualitative.

- **Incidence** is the number of new cases.
- **Prevalence** is the total number of cases.
- Predictive values depend on prevalence, whereas sensitivity/specificity does not.

- **Sensitivity** is TP/TP+FN

- **Specificity** is TN/TN+FP.

Common Abbreviations

a.a. – amino acid
AAA – abdominal aortic aneurysm
Ab – antibody
Abx – antibiotics
ACh – acetylcholine
ACT – activated clotting time
A-D – autosomal dominant
AdenoCa – adenocarcinoma
ADH – antidiuretic hormone
ADP – adenosine diphosphate
A.Fib – atrial fibrillation
AFP – alpha-fetoprotein
Ag – antigen
ALT – alanine aminotransferase
ALP – alkaline phosphatase
Ang – angiotensin
APR – abdominoperineal resection
A-R – autosomal recessive
ARDS – acute respiratory distress syndrome
ASA – acetylsalicylic acid
AST – aspartate aminotransferase
AT3 – antithrombin 3
ATN – acute tubular necrosis
ATP – adenosine triphosphate
A-V – arteriovenous
AVM – arteriovenous malformation
AVN – avascular necrosis
AZT – Zidovudine
B12 – vitamin B12
BM – bowel movement, basement membrane, bone marrow
BMI – body mass index
BP – blood pressure
Ca – cancer, carcinoma, Calcium
CABG – coronary artery bypass grafting
CAD – coronary artery disease
CBD – common bile duct
CCW – counterclockwise
CEA – carcio-embryonic antigen
CF – clotting factor
CGD – chronic granulomatous disease
CHF – congestive heart failure
Chole – cholecystectomy
Cl – chloride
CMV – cytomegalovirus

CN – cranial nerve
CNS – central nervous system
CO2 – carbon dioxide
COPD – chronic obstructive pulmonary disease
COX – cyclooxygenase
CPP – cerebral perfusion pressure
CRP – C-reactive protein
CSF – cerebral spinal fluid, colony-stimulating factor
CT – computed tomography, connective tissue
CVP – central venous pressure
Cx – culture
d/c – discharge, discontinue
DCIS – ductal carcinoma in-situ
DHFR – dihydrofolate reductase
DI – diabetes insipidus
DIC – disseminated intravascular coagulation
DM – diabetes mellitus
DPG – diphosphoglycerate
DPL – diagnostic peritoneal lavage
DVT – deep vein thrombosis
Dx – diagnose, diagnosis
E – epinephrine
EBV – Ebstein Barr virus
ECM – extracellular matrix
ECMO – extracorporeal membrane oxygenation
ED – emergency department
EGD – esophagogastroduodenoscopy
EJ – external jugular
EKG – electrocardiogram
ERCP – endoscopic retrograde cholangiopancreatography
F.A. – fatty acid
FAP – familial adenomatous polyposis
FAST – focused assessment with Sonography in trauma
FEV – forced expiratory volume
FFP – fresh frozen plasma
FGF – fibroblast growth factor
FN – false negative
FNA – fine needle aspiration
FP – false positive
FRC – functional residual capacity
Fru – fructose
FU – fluorouracil

137

G6PD – glucose-6-phospate dehydrogenase
Gala - galactose
GC – guanylyl cyclase
GCS – Glasgow coma scale
GE – gastroesophageal
GF – growth factor
GH – growth hormone
GI – gastrointestinal
Glu – glucose
GN – glomerulonephritis
GP – glycoprotein
H2O2 – hydrogen peroxide
Haemo – Haemophilus
HCC – hepatocellular carcinoma
hCG – human chorionic gonadotropin
HCO3 – bicarbonate
HDL – high density lipoprotein
Hep – hepatitis
His – Histamine
HOCl – hypochlorous acid
HIT – heparin-induced thrombocytopenia
HIV – human immunodeficiency virus
H&P – history and physical
HPF – high powered field
HPV – human papilloma virus
HR – heart rate
HSV – herpes simplex virus
HTN – hypertension
IBD – inflammatory bowel disease
ICP – intracranial pressure
ICU – intensive care unit
IF – intrinsic factor
IJ – internal jugular
IL – interleukin
IM – intramuscular
IMA – inferior mesenteric artery
IMV – inferior mesenteric vein
INF – interferon
INR – international normalized ratio
IV – intravenous
IVC – inferior vena cava
IVF – intravenous fluids
K – potassium
LAD – left anterior descending
Lap Chole – laparoscopic cholecystectomy
LBO – large bowel obstruction
LCIS – lobular carcinoma in-situ

LDL – low density lipoprotein
LMWH – low molecular weight heparin
LPL – lipoprotein lipase
LPS – lipopolysaccharide
LR – lactated ringer's
LV – left ventricle
MAC – minimum anesthetic concentration
MC – most common
MCly – most commonly
MCC – most common cause
MEN – multiple endocrine neoplasia
Mets – metastases
Mg – magnesium
MHC – major histocompatibility
MI – myocardial infarction
MRI – magnetic resonance imaging
Na – sodium
NE – norepinephrine
NEC – necrotizing enterocolitis
NF – neurofibromatosis
NG – nasogastric
NGT – nasogastric tube
NK – natural killer
NO – nitrous oxide
NPO – nothing per os
NS – normal saline
NSAID – non-steroidal anti-inflammatory drug
NSE – neuron specific enolase
n/v – nausea/vomiting
02 – Oxygen
OB – obstetrics
OCP – oral contraceptive pill
OR – operating room
ORIF – open reduction internal fixation
PABA – para-aminobenzoic acid
PCN – penicillin
PCWP – pulmonary capillary wedge pressure
PDA – patent ductus arteriosus, posterior descending artery
PDE – phosphodiesterase
PDGF – platelet derived growth factor
PE – pulmonary embolus
PEEP – positive end expiratory pressure
Perf - perforation
PET – positron emission tomography
PG – prostaglandin
PKD – polycystic kidney disease

PLC – Phospholipase C
PMN – polymorphonucleocyte
PNS – peripheral nervous system
PPD – purified protein derivative
PPI – proton-pump inhibitor
PPN – peripheral parenteral nutrition
PT – prothrombin time
PTA – percutaneous transluminal angioplasty
PTLD – posttransplant lymphoproliferative disease
PTT – partial thromboplastin time
PTU – propylthiouracil
RA – rheumatoid arthritis
RBC – red blood cell
RCC – renal cell carcinoma
RF – risk factor
RHD – rheumatic heart disease
RPR – rapid plasma reagin
RQ – respiratory quotient
RR – respiratory rate
RUQ – right upper quadrant
RV – residual volume
SBO – small bowel obstruction
SBP – spontaneous bacterial peritonitis
SCC – squamous cell carcinoma
SCM – sternocleidomastoid
SIADH – syndrome of inappropriate ADH secretion
SIRS – systemic inflammatory response syndrome
SLE – systemic lupus erythematous
SMA – superior mesenteric artery
SMV – superior mesenteric vein
SOD – superoxide dismutase
s/p – status post
Staph – Staphylococcus
STD – sexually transmitted disease
Strep – Streptococcus
SVC – superior vena cava
SVT – supraventricular tachycardia
T1/2 – half life
TB – tuberculosis
TBG – thyroid binding globulin
TBW – total body water
Tc cell – cytotoxic T-cell
TEF – transesophageal fistula
TF – transcription factor
TG – triglyceride
TGF – tissue growth factor

Th cell – helper T-cell
THF – tetrahydrofolate
TN – true negative
TNF – tumor necrosis factor
TP – true positive
tPA – tissue plasminogen activator
TPN – total parenteral nutrition
Tx – treat, treatment
TxA2 – thromboxane A2
U.C. – ulcerative colitis
UGI – upper G.I.
URTI – upper respiratory tract infection
U/S – ultrasound
UTI – urinary tract infection
V.Fib – ventricular fibrillation
VIP – vasoactive intestinal peptide
Vit – vitamin
VLDL – very low density lipoprotein
VMA – vanillylmandelic acid
VSD – ventricular septal defect
vWF – von Willebrand factor
VZV – varicella zoster virus
WBC – white blood count
XR – X-Ray
X-R – X-recessive

Amino Acids

Alanine – Ala
Arginine – Arg
Asparagine – Asn
Aspartic acid – Asp
Cysteine – Cys
Glutamic acid – Glu
Glutamine – Gln
Glycine – Gly
Histidine – His
Isoleucine – Ile
Leucine – Leu
Lysine – Lys
Methionine – Met
Phenylalanine – Phe
Proline – Pro
Serine – Ser
Threonine – Thr
Tryptophan – Trp
Tyrosine – Tyr
Valine – Val

Index

Lightning Source UK Ltd.
Milton Keynes UK
05 July 2010
156594UK00001B/19/P